Current Trends and Traditions in Management Accounting Case Analysis

Sixth Edition

Gary Spraakman

CAPTUS PRESS

Current Trends and Traditions in
    Management Accounting Case Analysis, Sixth edition

© 2015 by Gary Spraakman and Captus Press Inc.

First edition, Summer 1994
Sixth edition, Winter 2015

Captus Press Inc.
Mail: Units 14 & 15
        1600 Steeles Avenue West
        Concord, Ontario
        Canada L4K 4M2
Telephone: (416) 736–5537
Fax: (416) 736–5793
E-mail: info@captus.com
Internet: www.captus.com

Library and Archives Canada Cataloguing in Publication

Spraakman, Gary, author
        Current trends and traditions in management accounting
case analysis / Gary Spraakman. — 6th ed.

Includes bibliographical references.
ISBN 978-1-55322-323-8

    1. Managerial accounting — Case studies. I. Title

HF5657.4.S67 2015   658.15'11   C2014-907579-0

Canada ▮▮▮ *We acknowledge the financial support of the
Government of Canada through the Canada
Book Fund (CBF) for our publishing activities.*

0 9 8 7 6 5 4 3 2 1
Printed in Canada

Contents

Assg # 1 ✓

I have many people to thank. Let me start with my students who deserve special thanks for allowing me to test these cases. I learn much from them. I thank the many professors who have adopted the various editions of this casebook. A special thanks goes to Professor Lawrence Shum. My family has been very helpful in proofing reading my many cases. Thank you Cherilyn, Christopher, Andrea, and Sylvie. And, thank you Pauline Lai — you allow me to brag to my colleagues that I have the best editor.

This book of cases is directed at students who are taking a course in management accounting. It seeks to get students to think as management accountants. The materials presuppose introductory courses in management accounting and financial accounting.

As a supplement to management accounting textbooks, this book has six purposes. The first two are typical and related:

1. To supply cases that demand the application of management accounting techniques.
2. To introduce students to more practical situations than those typical of most textbooks.

The next two purposes differentiate this casebook from others:

3. To provide material that keeps abreast of changes to practice.
4. To familiarize students with the traditions of case analysis in management accounting.

The cases included in this book respond to the difficulties students experience when case analysis is demanded of them. I believe their difficulties occur for a number of reasons:

• Students spend up to 50 percent of their time reading and digesting the material before they do any thinking and writing. It is as if case authors advocate using long cases as teaching devices in order to allow adequate data for decision making, but the effort required to digest the case may leave the student little time for in-depth analysis.

• The case approach is learned, but not taught. Many students are forced to learn the case approach in a very general and imprecise fashion, almost like osmosis.

• Although students can identify issues or problems, they have difficulty with analysis; i.e., they have trouble discerning related themes, causes, and effects among issues, which is the objective of case analysis.

• Recommendations are readily suggested, but they are neither explained nor justified. When cases require implementation planning, recommendations are outlined in the most rudimentary fashion.

• Case responses tend to display a superficial understanding of case questions. This is probably a result of the other weaknesses and not a separate weakness.

I believe these weaknesses have two roots. First, the teaching of the case approach is implicit, and case analysis skills appear elusive to students. Second, long, verbose cases encourage superficial thinking because there is insufficient time for in-depth considerations.

These weaknesses, and my desire to remove them, suggest the final two purposes of this book:

5. To provide short cases so as to minimize reading time and to encourage greater depth of analysis.
6. To teach case analysis explicitly and provide feedback for learning.

This is an exciting time in which to design a management accounting casebook. Management accounting is in a period of transition. Since 1987 when Johnson and Kaplan (1987) called attention to the stagnation of management accounting practices, there have been many changes, such as activity-based costing and target costing. During the past decade an increasing number of companies have been impacted by information technology in terms of computerized transaction processing and electronic telecommunications, such as that done with the Internet, intranet, and extranet. For competitive reasons, companies have had to change from manual and then mainframe systems to what have been called enterprise resource planning (ERP) systems. An ERP system has a common database or data warehouse that links together all systems in all parts of a company, including, for example, capital budgeting with financial, control, manufacturing, sales, fixed assets, inventory, human resources modules, etc. By linking all systems through a data warehouse, ERP systems allow a company to manage its operations holistically.

A second impact of ERP systems has been a general shift to manage at the activity level rather than at the more abstract level of financial transactions. This means that management accounting, with its focus on activities, can be most effective when it is used with ERP systems to incorporate the activity level for costing and performance measurement. To be effective an ERP system will contain an extensive chart of accounts or codes for activities such as accurate recording and tracking of activities, revenues and costs. The coding incorporates stable entities of a business, such as divisions, plants, stores, and warehouses. At a detailed level there are codes for functions such as finance, production, sales, marketing, and materials management. There are also the traditional financial account codes, such as assets, liabilities, revenues, and expenses, and the central ERP feature of coding processes, activities, and sub-activities. There must be consistent coding among all parts of a company in order for them to relate to one another.

As the ERP system incorporates activities in terms of quantities of resources, including labour, a record of resource use is maintained. Therefore, performance can be measured in physical terms and compared to standards, which allows for the calculation of variances. This performance measurement at the activity level serves as a feedback system on efficiency and effectiveness. The confusion caused by abstract monetary measures is erased, and what is actually happening with the conversion of resources into goods and services can be seen. ERP systems have the potential to change management accounting systems with more detailed, more integrated, and faster produced information.

The information technology context of contemporary organizations has been incorporated into many of the cases contained in this book, which has two sections.

Section I describes management accounting case analysis for students. It contains Chapters 1, 2, and 3. Chapters 1 and 2 explain how students can develop judgment or, in other words, learn case analysis through two parts: (i) how to think like a management accountant and (ii) a framework for learning and teaching management accounting. Chapter 3 furthers the instructions for learning management accounting by providing a practice case complete with a suggested solution and by explaining how cases are marked.

Section II contains 39 cases for demonstrating and for assessment of students. These cases are designed for developing case analysis skills in students. Six new cases have been added, and two have been deleted. All of the cases have been class-tested. They are set in various industries: manufacturing, mining, service, non-profit, and government. Taken together, the cases cover most of the traditional management accounting techniques discussed at the introductory or intermediate levels of management accounting. They also include contemporary management accounting techniques, such as balanced scorecard, cost of quality report, performance measurement, value chain, business models, customer relationship management, enterprise resource planning systems, and outsourcing.

SECTION I

The Case Approach

## CHAPTER 1

Developing Judgment

Management accounting case analysis or, in other words, to think like a management accountant is both teachable and learnable. Case analysis involves the use of judgment in complex practical situations in regard to the identification and analyses of issues, the choice of appropriate techniques for analyzing the issues, and recommendations for resolving the issues. Issues, analyses, and recommendations are the focus of this chapter. The techniques needed for case analysis will have been learned in management accounting courses.

DEFINITION OF A CASE

Students need to begin with a clear understanding of the case analysis method. Mauffette-Leenders et al. (1997: 2) define a case as

> a description of an actual situation, commonly involving a decision, a challenge, an opportunity, a problem, or an issue faced by a person (or persons) in an organization. The case allows you to step figuratively into the position of a particular decision maker.

The written description of the practical situation is called the "case question". A good case question offers as real a practice situation as can be achieved short of the "real thing". It puts students at the scene of the action and familiarizes them with the actors and the contexts for their actions.

There are four objectives with the case method; awareness of these objectives will help students understand the process of case analysis.

OBJECTIVE 1: To help the student learn to put management accounting techniques such as budgeting and variance analysis into practice.

OBJECTIVE 2: To turn the student into an active learner rather than simply a passive accumulator of information. Case analysis helps students to acquire the habit of diagnosing issues, analyzing and evaluating alternatives, and formulating workable plans of action to resolve the issues.

OBJECTIVE 3: To train students to work out answers for themselves, rather than relying upon the authority of the professor or a textbook.

OBJECTIVE 4: To provide students with exposure to a range of organizations and management accounting situations, which otherwise would take a lifetime of experience to acquire. The exposure to a variety of situations will help students make career choices, as well as assist them in their careers.

This chapter will examine two interdependent approaches to learning case analysis. The first approach provides very detailed steps in writing case responses. The second approach places case analysis in the broader context of learning management accounting. Together the two approaches can provide students with the tools for effectively learning management accounting case analysis.

1. WRITING CASE RESPONSES

Understanding the educational objectives of the case approach will help students pursue these assignments effectively. The case objectives come from Bloom's taxonomy (Bloom et al., 1956), which has long been accepted by accounting educators (Clevenger, 1990).

Following are Bloom's educational objectives:

1. **Knowledge**. Recalling previously learned material. Students need to remember facts, principles, and steps in a sequence. A sample question that seeks out student knowledge would be, "Define variable and fixed costs."

2. **Comprehension**. The understanding of material presented in a course. At this level students explain, interpret, translate to a new form or symbol system, and extrapolate. A sample question would be, "Explain an operating statement along the lines of variable costing."

3. **Application**. The ability to use learning in other situations. Students are to use abstractions such as concepts, principles, rules, theories, techniques, and laws to find solutions to new problems. A sample question would be, "Use the contribution margin technique to explain the level of sales needed to break even." Numerical exercises and problems at the back of management accounting textbook chapters tend to be applications.

4. **Analysis**. The capability for breaking content into component parts in order to understand the relationships among parts. A sample question would be, "Compare and contrast the operating statement for the company under absorption costing with direct costing."

5. **Synthesis**. Putting together of parts to form a new whole. Students use what they have learned to produce new products, such as themes, speeches, or research proposals. A sample question would be, "From the evidence in the case, discuss how, with an expansionary, high-end-of-the-market strategy, the company became bankrupt."

6. **Evaluation**. The ability to judge the value of material in light of a specific purpose using given criteria. Students make quantitative and qualitative judgments about the extent to which material and methods satisfy criteria.

A sample question would be, "Using the criteria of relevant and timely information for making decisions, evaluate the division's new information system compared to that which existed previously."

The case approach for management accounting presupposes that students possess a high degree of knowledge, comprehension and application skills, the first three of the six ascending educational objectives in the taxonomy. The primary focus of the case approach for this book is on analysis and synthesis.

An example of a response that reveals analysis skills might be one in which the student considers the operating statements of an organization in comparison to the industry and realizes "the organization is performing more poorly than the industry average."

More specifically, the student would exhibit analytical skill if he or she determined the following:

- The contribution of all 12 sales regions.
- Eight of the 12 sales regions were profitable, and four were not.
- The unprofitable sales regions were in remote parts of the country, with higher turnover, especially among managers. Apparently, these remote managers did not consider themselves truly part of the firm.
- Few managers of the unprofitable regions had promotions to corporate office jobs.

Synthesis builds upon analysis and it asks, "What does it all mean?" Continuing with our example, a student could synthesize the evidence to explain that the poor profitability in the remote sales areas is a result of poor motivation, caused by the organization's neglect of the remote sales areas. As a consequence of this neglect, there is a higher than average turnover, and the managers do not believe themselves to be integral parts of the company. Synthesis is the skill by which evidence is linked together, creating a plausible explanation.

2. RESPONDING TO A CASE QUESTION

This sub-section will discuss the component parts of the case method and the student's responsibilities. The focus of this sub-section will be on helping the student to respond appropriately to a case question. As well, this section will provide some practical "how to" advice. Based on the suggestions in this sub-section, and with practice, students should be able to develop their initial approach to case analysis that they are comfortable applying in various case question situations.

There are two components to case analysis: the case question and the case response.

Case Question

The case question establishes the scenario or "story" of an organization. Typically, it includes characters — managers, workers, customers, etc. — and a setting that will be some part or perspective of an organization. Cases can depict any type of organization, and there are many possible scenarios, given the number of management accounting topics and the equally large number of organizational types.

No matter what the management accounting scenario, there are issues (or problems) that must be resolved. An issue exists when there is a gap between expectations and actual performance in an area of an organization. For example, management accounting teaches students that organizations should have budgets for operational guidance. When a scenario states that an organization does not have a budget, then this is an issue.

The scenario of a case question will generally contain many issues revealed in comments made by case actors, findings by case actors, trends or ratios contained in financial statements, financial summaries, industry comparisons, etc. Identification of issues at first may be difficult. Through practice, however, students will become proficient at identifying, as well as linking, them.

One way to identify issues is to determine those attributes of the hypothetical organization that differ from the accounting and management practices that are taught as good practice. Another method is to identify those attributes that lead to less than optimal economic performance. Examples include declining sales in comparison to those of competitors, missed profit opportunities, managers insufficiently profit-oriented, inaccurate budgeting, misleading cost accounting, ineffective sales incentives, and a failure to develop replacements for maturing products, etc.

Imagine a case where two managers did not get along personally: a lumber manufacturing organization's log purchasing manager and mill manager refused to co-operate with each other. Their inability to co-operate led to a shortage of appropriate logs for a certain large and important order, and caused other production scheduling problems as well. There are three issues in this example. First, personal conflict was affecting operations. Second, scheduling difficulties occurred. Third, management was unable to develop the necessary systems for scheduling that would work despite personal conflicts. For this example, the *root* issue was that "management was not able to develop the necessary systems." The other two issues, "personal conflict" and "scheduling deficiencies", are due to the lack of appropriate systems. With proper systems for scheduling that would work despite personal conflicts, "personal conflict" and "scheduling deficiencies" would not be problematic.

In addition to the scenario, the case question may contain a "required" that asks the student to do something. Typically, the "required" is the link between the case question and the case response. A required can be directed or non-directed, depending on the amount of direction provided to the student. Students should take special care to correctly understand the "required" before formulating the case response.

Learning to read a case efficiently and effectively is the key to good case analysis. Students should develop approaches that suit their typical reading strategies. Nevertheless, a recommended approach is to read the case quickly in order to get a sense of the context, and then to re-read it carefully and in detail. If one uses this approach, it is advisable to read the "required" before the second reading of the case. Re-reading with the "required" in mind allows one to discriminate between what is essential in the case and what is not.

Case Response

The case response is the student's answer to the case question. There is no one right or definitive answer to a case question. However, a student should not conclude that there are no wrong answers. Case responses differ because of differing identification of issues and analysis of relations among issues, differing determinations of what the root or underlying issues are, and differing development of recommendations to resolve the root issues and, in turn, the other issues. Although a variety of responses are valid at every stage, some, clearly, are incorrect.

The case response format is not fixed; typically it depends on the case question. However, using a simple, standardized form will improve case responses and provide a context for unambiguous marking. It is recommended that students use the issue–analyses–recommendations framework, deciding for themselves, according to the particular case, whether to use the three headings or to combine the first and second or the second and third. The three parts are described and analyzed below.

Issues

Problems or issues are those attributes, factors, and/or activities that are wrong with the organization.

Students should read a case question once or twice to gather its essence. While reading, it is helpful to identify the issues by circling or highlighting them or by taking notes. Then, the student reviews these identified issues, adding to them any issues revealed by related analysis of financial statements and other supplementary information supplied.

In order to "size up" the root issues, it is essential to have a clear understanding of the organization and its issues. This analysis can be accomplished in two steps.

First, make a list of the issues. Arrange and assemble similar issues into groups. Explain the relationships among the groups or categories that emerge at this stage. The groupings should be governed by two criteria. First, same or related issues should be grouped together; for example, all issues related to inaccurate financial information would go into one group. Second, associations among issues within a group should be specified; for example, inaccurate accounting information led to poor decisions on inventory orders.

Second, the relationship among the categories must be explained. This explanation should reveal the root issues. Once they are disclosed, the root issues should be linked in a logical sequence. This listing should show the dependent relationship between the other issues and their root issues. Care should be taken to account for any specific requests that arise because of the role assigned to the student. The request may specify the perspective the student takes in assessing the issues. Requests may also be understood as additional issues.

The primary reason for grouping and ranking issues is to detect the underlying pattern of root issues. Sometimes, issues may also be the same as the root issues. In others, the detection may be more difficult. For example, consider a manufacturing firm with several problems: sales are not growing as expected; customers are returning products; customer satisfaction with the product quality is declining; and rework has increased. The root issue, lack of quality control, causes the other issues. Specifically, there was no quality control in the production process. The absence of quality control led to more rework and to the shipping of defective products, which the customers then returned or refused to buy again, and persuaded others not to buy.

It is identification of the root issues that enables the student to specify succinctly what is wrong with an organization. Proper identification requires close reading of the entire case, including appendices. Some information may have little or no bearing on the issues. As in the real-life situations that case analysis seeks to emulate, the student must sift carefully through all discernible aspects of a situation in order to determine what is relevant.

Analysis

Analysis and issue identification are highly related. Analysis requires a thorough assessment of why an issue arose or exists, how various issues relate to each other, and which issues lead to others and are, therefore, the most crucial to an understanding of the root issues. The analysis section includes required quantitative analysis, e.g., cost–volume–profit variance analysis. The analysis discloses how well essential organizational functions are working, e.g., planning, controlling, and management information systems. Analysis can also reveal, when necessary, the strengths and weaknesses of the organization. The analysis may vary in complexity. It can be as simple as listing the supporting issues, or as complex as finding the root or underlying issues.

Some case questions have a singular answer either because of the context or because of the "required". Other case questions lend themselves to a series of alternatives for solving issues. Alternatives should be individually meaningful and mutually exclusive. For example, for a business with serious profit problems, one alternative might be to reduce costs and focus on the core business. Another alternative might be to close the business and sell the assets and inventories. Each alternative must be explained and justified as an answer, and if appropriate, its advantages and disadvantages should be discussed.

Recommendations

The recommendations are a student's approach to remedying the root issues. If there are alternatives, the recommendations should be selected from the alternatives discussed in the analysis section. In resolving the root issues, the recommendations must also resolve most of the other issues. Recommendations should be action oriented, decisive and unambiguous; i.e., they should explicitly resolve the issues, assign responsibilities and set deadlines.

It may be suitable to include a conclusion that deals with implementation, especially with timing, and the assignment of responsibilities that arise out of the recommendations.

For example, with respect to the organization with profit problems, a student might recommend cost cutting and focus on the core business alternative. The student should follow the selection of this alternative by specifying how he or she would resolve the profit problems, and by suggesting an implementation plan. The implementation should detail which costs are to be cut, by whom, and with what consequences. It should detail which businesses are to be eliminated and which ones are to remain. If sufficient information is available, the recommendations should be quantified, showing the expected profit improvement.

In the report writing stage, it is often more time efficient and effective to identify, analyze, and make recommendations for each root issue individually. It is nevertheless essential to show the integration of the various issues within the case. Whatever the approach, it should be justified as the most appropriate for the case question.

Types of Cases

Cases can be differentiated according to three characteristics: (1) the extent to which the "required" directs students, (2) the number of possible correct responses, and (3) the number of management accounting techniques evoked by the analysis. These characteristics are often interrelated.

A case's "required" can be directed or non-directed. A directed case leaves little opportunity for the student to decide the issues that need addressing, e.g., "calculate the net present value of a capital project." A non-directed case is just the opposite. Students must determine the issues, e.g., "make recommendations to improve profitability."

The degree of directness of the "required" often relates to the number of possible correct responses. Generally, in non-directed cases, students can choose more than one way of seeing or grouping the issues, and so will arrive at a variety of appropriate sets of issues–analyses–recommendations. Consequently, there probably will be many correct responses, or solutions. At the other extreme, in a directed case, there are a restricted number of correct responses, possibly only one.

The number of management accounting techniques incorporated into a case can vary from as few as two to as many as 10 or 12. As a rule, the more techniques that are used, the larger the number of possible acceptable responses is, and the less directed the case is.

This book consists largely of directed cases, each employing two or three management accounting techniques, and inviting several possible correct responses. This level of complexity is appropriate for intermediate management accounting students, and it is a step towards preparing students for minimally directed, multi-technique cases with many possible correct responses.

Writing the Case Response

The role that the student is to play is usually established in the case question, sometimes in the "required". Also specified will be for whom the student is working. For example, the student may be a controller working closely with the president to determine funding for a capital project. As controller, the student must write a report to the president.

The case response in this context is prepared as a report. Typically it contains an introduction, and sections for issues, analysis, recommendations, and conclusion. The student should include a covering memorandum transmitting the report from the role played to the person or position for whom the work is being done. A short paragraph noting that the report is enclosed and linking it with the "required" is usually in order.

The Role of the Student

The essence of the student's role in case analysis is to diagnose and size up an organization's situation and to think through what, if anything, should be done. The student identifies and analyzes the root issue(s) and other issues, and proposes recommendations to resolve them. In formulating their analyses and recommendations, students must make assumptions about how the issues relate to one another. Assumptions must be realistic, given the context of the question.

After reading this section, it is important for students to recognize that cases will differ. Understanding the differences will enable students to be successful with case analysis. For the level of case analysis intended with this book, there are three ways of differentiating cases.

First, cases can be differentiated as to educational objective. Students will be tested for analysis or synthesis. Analysis requires students to break content into component parts and then to understand the relationships among those parts. Alternatively, synthesis requires students to take the parts to form a new whole. A case could test students for their ability to undertake analysis or synthesis, or both. Of course, for the management accounting techniques for which they are responsible, students must be competent as to the educational objectives of knowledge, comprehension, and application.

Second, cases can be differentiated by the number of issues, which could vary from a few to many. All issues must be considered, either on their own or by grouping or synthesis. Thus, cases with more issues tend to be more demanding than cases with fewer issues.

Third, cases differ by the directedness of the "required". Directed cases tend to be easier for students.

This casebook contains cases that tend to need analysis and synthesis. They contain relatively few issues, and they tend to be directed.

## CHAPTER 2

Learning Management Accounting Case Analysis

The first part of this chapter explains how to think like a management accountant. Then the second part discusses a framework for learning/teaching management accounting. This framework comes from my teaching of management accounting, writing cases and reviewing cases for publication, and my research. The framework was developed from a pertinent mathematical framework with a fellow accounting academic, Professor Beverley Jackling of Victoria University, Australia.[1]

You may ask, why do students and instructors need a framework? The justification for a framework is to have a systematic set of premises based on empirical evidence of how students learn to think and behave as management accountants. Without such a framework instructors may not be following teaching practices that contribute efficiently and effectively to student learning. Likely, all instructors have frameworks in their minds when teaching case analysis. More likely, those frameworks are undocumented and ad hoc, and certain parts may be inconsistent with other parts. In contrast, a documented framework is more likely to be internally consistent and open to criticism and, subsequently, to improvement through evidence. Consequently, improving the process of learning/teaching management accounting is more difficult without a documented framework.

I could not find any theories or frameworks for learning/teaching management accounting. However, I recognized that management accounting uses mathematical calculations, which may be financial or non-financial. A literature search revealed that Schoenfeld (1985) had developed a framework to explain how mathematicians think, which was found to be appropriate for learning/teaching management accounting. Professor Jackling and I adapted Schoenfeld's (1985) mathematical framework to learning/teaching management accounting. The adapted framework retained the four key components from Schoenfeld (1985) — resources, techniques, control, and beliefs — which will be described for learning/teaching management accounting.

---

1. This subsection draws heavily upon Spraakman and Jackling (2014).

Resources

This is the inventory of management accounting facts and procedures accessible to the students. These resources are mainly the materials presented in management accounting textbooks. Typically, management accounting textbooks are organized by topic-based chapters, which can be divided into two parts: text materials and end-of-chapter assessment materials. The text materials provide thorough backgrounds or resources. Although there is excessive detail for standard problems at the end-of-chapter exercises and problems, the nuanced descriptions and explanations in the text materials equip students to do non-standard problems or cases. An example of text resources would be the discussion of variance analysis in Chapter 7 of Horngren et al.'s *Cost Accounting: A Managerial Emphasis* (2013). Horngren et al. define a variance as the difference between actual results and expected performance and then demonstrate how numerous variances are calculated with flexible budgeting. In Chapter 7, Horngren et al. also describe how the flexible budget is based on standard costs and demonstrate the respective journal entries of a standard costing system and the management use of variance analysis.

Resources also include other course materials, including the instructor's lectures and the respective slides, supplementary cases and readings, discussions with fellow students, work experiences, and course pre-requisites.

Techniques

Management accounting numerically based heuristics or techniques are carefully defined and carefully taught. An example of a technique would be the contribution margin, which, as noted, is revenues less variable costs. Another example of a technique is capital budgeting, which discounts cash flows for assessing long term investment decisions.

To demonstrate technique, a breakeven analysis can be used as an example. The breakeven point refers to the sales level at which sales minus variable costs equals fixed costs. This technique tends to be discussed in textbook chapters covering cost–volume–profit analysis — e.g., Chapter 3 of Horngren et al. (2013) — and it is reinforced with exercises and problems at the end-of-chapter. In other words, the breakeven analysis is a resource, as it is discussed in the text material in the chapter, but it becomes a technique in the exercises and problems provided for practice in the end-of-chapter materials.

Another example of a management accounting technique is variance analysis in Chapter 7 of Horngren et al. (2013). The variance analysis technique is called a performance report or level 2 variance analysis, as shown Exhibit 2.1.

The performance report explicitly calculates the variances for flexible-budget, sales volume, and static budget. It also enables numerous other variances to be calculated, e.g. price variances, efficiency variances. The exercises and problems at the end of the chapters test students in applying the performance report to different sets of data. For example, exercise 7-23 in Horngren et al. (2013) provides the basic performance report but with only the data for static budget and actual results columns; students are to calculate the missing fields in the remaining four columns.

In Schoenfeld's terms (1985), the mathematical exercises and problems at the end of the chapters with single answers would be considered standard problems, whereas cases with multiple possible answers would be considered non-standard problems. A problem is non-standard when, as described by Schoenfeld, "the students will not be able to solve them by simply recalling and applying familiar solution patterns."

EXHIBIT 2.1
Standard Problem

Performance Report

	Actual Results	Flexible-Budget Variances	Flexible-Budget	Sales-Volume Variances	Static Budget
	(1)	(2) = (1) – (3)	(3)	(4) = (3) – (5)	(5)
Units sold (000s of units)	10	0	10	2U	12
Revenues ($000s)	1,250	50	1,200	240 U	1,440
Variable costs					
Direct materials	622	22	600	120 F	720
Direct manufacturing labour	198	38	160	32 F	192
Variable manufacturing overhead	130	10	120	24 F	144
Total variable costs	950	70	880	176 F	1,056
Contribution margin	300	20	320	64 U	384
Fixed manufacturing costs	285	9	276	0	276
Operating income	15	29	44	64 U	108
Level 2	^	$29U	^	$64 U	^
		Flexible-budget variance		Sales volume variance	
Level 1	^		$93U		^
			Static-budget variance		

Source: Horngren et al. (2009), p. 229.

Problem solving requires the use of management accounting techniques that, as noted, are comparable to Schoenfeld's heuristics.

Techniques are established methods for solving management accounting problems. Problems are explicitly or implicitly stated in mathematical terms; a mathematical management accounting technique solves the problem. Consider the following two additional examples of management accounting techniques:

- *Absorption costing.* This is a technique where the fixed manufacturing costs and certain variable costs are charged to the cost of goods sold to indicate cost.

- *Cost–volume–profit analysis.* With the contribution margin as the denominator, this technique specifies the sales volume needed to cover the predetermined fixed costs, and perhaps income taxes and profits.

Management accounting techniques are explicit in exercises or standard problems. For example, the standard problem requires students to learn and apply the heuristic with different sets of data. As such, the technique operates at Bloom et al.'s (1956) third level of educational objectives, application. Bamber and Bamber (2006: 278) say most end-of-chapter exercises and problems do not challenge students beyond application.

Cases (i.e., non-standard problems) are those to which a technique or techniques cannot be automatically applied. The matching of the appropriate technique or techniques with the issue or issues is not straight forward. There is not a single match as with a standard problem; there are many possible matches. Interpretation and critical thinking are needed prior to matching; that is, it may be necessary to undertake analysis or synthesis as specified by Bloom et al. (1956) as higher level educational objectives. With analysis, the breaking of the issue or issues into parts may reveal opportunities for appropriate use of techniques. Similarly, synthesis by putting the parts together in a different way may also reveal opportunities for the use of techniques. In other words, case analysis requires the restating of the issues with analysis and synthesis. My assumption that management accounting cases require higher levels of cognitive skills than standard numerical problems is attested to by Bonner (1999: 31–32, 37) and Ballantine and McCourt Larres (2004: 186–187).

Control

Schoenfeld (1985) recognizes that it is not only the available or known resources and techniques, but also "competent decision-making [that] is necessary for success." Control refers to how management accounting practitioners or students select and deploy available resources and techniques. Control is concerned with matching techniques with the issues for a resolution.

Briefly, control would require a number of steps, such as careful assessment or reading of the management accounting case; reviewing pertinent resources; considering the possible techniques that match or, in other words, could be used to solve the apparent issues; implementing the technique most appropriate to solve the issue or issues; and reviewing the results against the original issue or issues to ensure there was a solution. If not successful, start again from the beginning.

Control, as noted, refers to how issue solvers select and deploy available resources and techniques. With standard problems, the challenge is not great: simple matching is required, and the control comes into play when the student has learned to apply the techniques.

Control is less straight forward with cases, and that is why the "case approach" is used, with a format such as issues–analysis–recommendations. There are other formats. Nevertheless, the case approach, by providing "reflection and learning", can be thought of as a metaphor for problem-based learning (Greenhalgh, 2007: 185).

Belief Systems

The management accounting world views determine the effectiveness of the case analysis. These views enable the bringing together of resources, techniques, and control. Only these prevailing common beliefs will allow students to excel with case analysis. Below are some examples of management accounting beliefs:

- A neo-classical economic foundation; more revenues and more profits are desirable; less costs and less expenses are also desirable.
- A financial accounting foundation provided by double-entry bookkeeping systems; all financial accounting information can be reconciled through debits and credits.
- Inputs are reconciled with outputs; complete tracking is required.
- Managers make decisions with management accounting information.
- Non-financial information is an insightful alternative to the more abstract financial accounting information (Schwartz et al., 2006; Blocher, 2009).

To make techniques, resources, and controls work effectively, students (as with practitioners) need to believe in the validity of management accounting information for assisting managers to plan, make decisions, evaluate performance, and control an organization. In addition to believing in management accounting, it is necessary to trust the managers to be effective in using that information. The most important belief is that information as provided by management accounting is useful for the purposes intended.

Application of the Framework

Consider the case captured with Exhibit 2.2. There are three parts to the table in the exhibit: an operating statement with actual annual results, a budget, and variances between actual and budget; the summary results from cost of quality reports for the years T_{-5} to T; and the summary results of customer satisfaction reports for six years. The operating statement in the first part of Exhibit 2.2 resembles the performance report technique in Exhibit 2.1. The technique, as noted earlier, is explained in Chapter 7 of Horngren et al. (2013). The cost of quality report in the second part of the table is from the technique by the same name in Chapter 19 of Horngren et al. (2013); this report accumulates all costs to do with product quality, the costs incurred in generating quality or from lacking of quality. The third part of the table in Exhibit 2.2 contains another technique from Chapter 8 of Horngren et al. (2013), customer satisfaction reporting with various attributes of the company's products.

The numerical information in Exhibit 2.2 is one of two types of information provided to students in management accounting cases. The other is narrative information (Gobeil and Phillips, 2001); the following quotation from the case question contains typical but brief narrative information that supplements the students' understanding of the numerical information in Exhibit 2.2.

> The company tied to [Exhibit 2.2] is a manufacturer of quality household furniture. In the past year, two changes were introduced. The company contracted out more production to reduce costs and it added more product finishes to meet customer demand. With the contracting out production, the company made quality control the responsibility of the contractors. Warranty work is charged to manufacturing overhead. Operating income has declined by nearly 60 percent from what was expected. You are required to determine the reasons for the decline in operating income and recommend actions to improve operating income.

A case requires students to match the issue or issues underlying Exhibit 2.2 and the above quotation with sense-making techniques. The students proceed to match issues with techniques in the belief that management accounting information (financial or non-financial) can solve such issues. The starting point with cases is the control, the case approach consisting of issues–analysis–recommendations. Students must have knowledge and understanding of the relevant techniques, as well as the resources and beliefs to enable the matching of techniques with issues. With the narrative, the operating statement in Exhibit 2.2 could be analyzed by students with the performance report technique in Exhibit 2.1. Although there are no units, students, after noting that budget and actual sales are basically the same, would assume that the actual mix and unit prices are the same as budget, and thus the performance report could be used. The variance analysis in Exhibit 2.2 equates to the performance report without a volume variance. The decline in operating income is largely attributed to variable and fixed overhead; the other variances are minor and often offsetting. The cost of quality report shows that in the recent year, there were reduced expenditures for prevention

EXHIBIT 2.2
Non-Standard Problem

Operating Statement
(For the year ending December 31, Year T, $000,000s)

	Budget	Actual	Variance
Revenues	$432.0	$436.6	$ 4.6
Cost of goods sold			
Variable costs:			
Materials	125.4	129.6	(4.2)
Manufacturing labour	21.2	22.8	(1.6)
Manufacturing overhead	47.4	50.2	(2.8)
Sales support	17.2	17.4	(0.2)
Total costs	211.2	220.0	(8.8)
Contribution margin	220.8	216.6	(4.2)
Fixed expenses:			
Manufacturing overhead	98.8	132.2	(33.4)
Sales overhead	21.4	21.2	0.2
Administration overhead	37.2	37.4	(0.2)
Total expenses	157.4	190.8	(33.4)
Operating income	$ 63.4	$ 25.8	$(37.6)

Cost of Quality Report
($ millions)

	Years					
	T	T_{-1}	T_{-2}	T_{-3}	T_{-4}	T_{-5}
Prevention	$ 2.2	$ 6.2	$ 6.4	$ 6.0	$5.6	$5.2
Inspections	0.2	2.6	2.8	2.4	2.0	2.0
Internal failure	4.2	2.2	2.0	1.4	1.6	1.6
External failure	13.6	1.2	0.4	1.2	0.6	0.8
Total	$20.2	$12.2	$11.6	$11.0	$9.8	$9.6

Customer Satisfaction
(Highly unsatisfied, 0%, to highly satisfied, 100%)

	Years					
	T	T_{-1}	T_{-2}	T_{-3}	T_{-4}	T_{-5}
Quality	61.5	85.5	84.7	85.9	86.1	85.3
Durability	58.3	93.3	92.7	92.2	92.7	93.6
Value for Money	48.6	75.1	77.5	76.6	78.1	76.4
Finishes	88.6	53.8	56.3	55.8	54.7	

and inspections (because quality control was delegated to suppliers) and increased outlays for internal and external failures, probably because product quality decreased. This is verified by the customer satisfaction decreasing for quality, durability, and value for money.

An explanation of the operating income decrease is that customers are less satisfied with their purchases of household furniture. The reduction in outlays for prevention and inspection can explain the increases in internal and external failure, which are reflected in more charges to manufacturing overhead. They also explain the reduction in customer satisfaction. These are the apparent issues, and their resolutions or recommendations are needed to improve product quality, durability, and value for money. The root issue is that products are now of poor quality. The recommendations are to improve product quality by increasing inspections to 100 percent, and by training and monitoring contractors to improve quality. Replacement of contractors that are not meeting quality standards is also required.

In summary, through matching of issues with techniques, students identify the root issue, which constitutes the first part of the control, the case format. The techniques enable the issues to be analyzed, synthesized or explained in cause and effect terms; this is the second part of the case approach. By analyzing the issues with heuristics, solutions or recommendations are generated. Christensen and Carlile (2009: 244) explain this as the relationship between the "descriptive theory" of analysis and "prescriptive theory" of the recommendations. Relatedly, Mauffette-Leenders et al. (1997: 3) — who provided us with our definition of cases — explain how cases contribute to student in-depth learning:

> [Cases] enable you to learn by doing and by teaching others. What you learn becomes deeply ingrained and stays with you. The repetitive opportunity to identify, analyze, and solve a number of issues in a variety of settings prepares you to become truly professional in your field of work ... Cases provide an opportunity to become deeply involved in decisions actually faced by real people in real organizations, to take ownership, to feel the pressure, to recognize the risks, and to expose your ideas to others.

CHAPTER 3

A Practice Case and Insights into Marking

As the title implies, this chapter provides a practice case and explains how cases are marked. Together these two parts further prepare students for case analysis.

A PRACTICE CASE

Case analysis is the application of management accounting techniques to practical issues. In simple cases, the issues and appropriate techniques are explicit. In more complex cases, the issues and appropriate techniques are harder to ascertain.

The casebook seeks to develop student skills for case analysis. The underlying premise is that instruction, coupled with practice and feedback, will produce expertise with case analysis. This practice case explicitly specifies in advance a management accounting technique to be applied to the case question. Normally, the student must determine the management accounting technique. However, by specifying the technique, this chapter explains how case questions are viewed from the perspective of a particular management accounting technique in determining issues.

Management Accounting Technique

For the case in this chapter, displayed in Exhibit 3.1, the management accounting technique will be "feedback information". This technique incorporates the belief that information on operations and employee behaviour will facilitate improvements to future performance. It is an underlying belief with financial and non-financial reports.

The case, PC Sales Division, is to be read, and it is to be assessed from the perspective of feedback information during the reading. This technique implies that feedback is useful and necessary if management is to be successful in directing employees. Consequently, the lack of feedback means that management is less than optimal, and issues have occurred or will occur because of the lack of feedback.

The Case Response

As noted, this is a short case set in a sales organization whose products are PCs and related equipment and software. The new sales manager has given his sales representa-

EXHIBIT 3.1
A Practice Case

PC Sales Division

You were a commissioned sales representative for five years. Although business was competitive, for three of those years you were the top sales representative for your company.

You thoroughly enjoyed your job. You had substantial independence. You selected the firms you wanted to contact. You determined the sales approach. There were no inhibiting rules or regulations. Your boss did not interfere, but instead bought you lunch every first Monday of the month. You did what you wanted to do because you were the top sales representative.

Fourteen months ago your boss retired, and you received his position as the sales manager, central division. Your subordinates include 24 commissioned sales persons, two order processing clerks, and a secretary/receptionist.

On the first day of your new job you made two commitments. First, you told your new boss, the VP of sales, that your unit's sales and profits would increase by 20 percent in the next year. Second, you gave the sales staff of your unit five steps that, if followed, would double their sales.

Now you regret those commitments. The first year has transpired. Sales are down 15 percent. Profits are down 25 percent. And rather than doubling sales, sales per sales person are down 10 percent, and three sales representatives have gone with a competitor.

In reflecting over the last year, your comments to the sales representatives keep coming back.

"The rules for successful selling are simple. By following my five rules, your personal sales will double and, with our commission structure, so will your gross income. My five rules are as follows:

1. Call all regular customers at least once every two weeks. Ask if they are planning to buy PCs, equipment, or software. Emphasize that you would be pleased to provide quotes.

2. New customers are essential for sales growth. Make 25 cold calls each month. Five should become new customers. I get company names from the telephone directories, trade directories, etc. With cold calls, I use the telephone and ask the answering receptionist for the person in charge of PC purchases. This usually leads to a few calls and questions before I reach the person most likely to be able to make purchases from us. I present myself, our company, and the fact that we supply and support PC compatible equipment and software.

3. I meet my active clients regularly. Clients with sales potential of less than $150,000 are met once a year. See clients twice a year if they have more potential.

4. Every month I send each active client something in the mail or through e-mail that keeps them aware of my name and telephone number.

5. I return all calls within an hour. This requires an answering service (no voice mail) and much cellular telephone activity.

With these steps I can work independently and effectively. I meet only once every month for lunch with my boss and all he does is to keep me informed about our new products."

These five steps have come to haunt you. All sales representatives have adamantly said they followed the five steps. They blame you for their failures. You do not know if they are telling the truth, or if they are not following the steps, or if your procedures are not effective for all sales representatives.

Very concerned with the decline in sales, the vice-president reviewed the five steps and admitted their validity. However, he suggested that they may not represent all the steps for successful selling. As an example, he mentioned that the content of discussions with clients and methods for closing a sale are important, but not included in the five steps. He also informed you that there have been complaints about sales representatives who compete with one another for the same orders.

You are confused. You know how to sell, but you do not know if your sales representatives know how.

Required

Using the case approach and the feedback information perspective, identify the root issues, analyze them, and make recommendations for resolving the issues.

tives instructions for successful selling. Despite explicit instructions, successful selling has not occurred. It is unclear why the selling has not been successful.

This is a directed case with a single technique, information theory. Consequently, there is expected to be a relatively narrow range of acceptable case responses.

Students must apply the described "information theory" to the case question. In reading the case, students readily detect, from available information, sales in aggregate are down 15 percent, profits are down 25 percent, etc. The five steps for improving sales by representatives are apparently not working, but there is no information on what steps work and what steps do not work. Moreover, there is no information on what steps work or do not work for the various sales representatives. Students will detect from information theory perspective that the new sales manager does not really know why the sales representatives are unsuccessful and that he needs information to indicate what they are doing wrong.

From the perspective of information theory, the root issue is that the sales manager does not know why the sales representatives are doing poorly. Analyzing the root issue reveals the consequences of not having information; e.g., the lack of information on the activities of sales representatives prevents the sales manager from knowing what they are doing, what they are not doing, what is successful, and what is not. Without this understanding, he does not know what to change, etc. The purpose of the analysis is (1) to convince the reader that the root issue is really the most important issue and (2) to lay the foundation for the recommendations.

The recommendations resolve the root issues. As the perspective for this case is information theory, the recommendations likely include developing an information system that tracks sales representative adherence to the five steps.

Exhibit 3.2 shows what a reasonable case response could look like.

EXHIBIT 3.2
A Sample Case Response

Case Response for PC Sales Division

Introduction
The sales of your unit have not increased as you expected after recommending the steps that worked for you.

Issues
The root issue is that you do not have information on how your recommended steps for selling are working.

Analyses
The lack of information has four parts.

1. You do not know if the steps are being followed.
2. You do not know if the steps if followed lead to the sales.
3. Your sales representatives do not know what is working and what is not.
4. There is no information on customer satisfaction with those steps.

Without information, you and your sales representatives are not able to change, add, and/or delete steps to increase sales effectiveness. Consequently, you are stuck with an approach which is apparently not working.

Recommendations
Develop an information system that tracks sales representative adherence to the steps, sales volume by sales representative, and customer satisfaction. This will allow you to know (i) if the steps are being followed and (ii) if followed, do they lead to more sales and more customer satisfaction.

INSIGHTS INTO MARKING

Understanding how cases are marked further clarifies the expectations underlying case analysis and thereby facilitates learning the case approach.

There are two basic approaches to marking cases: mechanical (or analytical) and subjective (or global or holistic). Mechanical marking involves identifying all possible attributes or aspects of a perfect answer and assigning a point value to each attribute. This is a thorough, detailed, rigid, and time-consuming approach to case marking. The other method is called subjective marking (or rating), which takes less time and is less detailed. Subjective marking involves identifying all root issues. Each response is judged as to how these root issues are addressed. With subjective marking each paper is generally marked twice. Significant differences between markers must be resolved. The advantage of subjective marking over mechanical marking is that it is not biased against short, uniquely insightful case responses. The lack of detail is its disadvantage.

Each method is discussed, with an example.

Mechanical Marking

As there is no singularly correct answer, mechanical marking must allow for all reasonable perceptions of the issues. To give credence to the expectation of more than one appropriate response, mechanical marking guides must have more marks than the total for the case question. For example, if there are 70 marks for a case question, the marking guide could have, say, 125 marks to recognize many possible correct responses. Seldom do students earn the full marks allotted because of limited time and because some marks overlap. Thus, any response justified with evidence in the case question will receive marks. There is another way to explain excess marks.

Case questions contain issues or evidence on root issues. However, the linkage between an issue and a root issue is not explicit. Students must argue the relationship. For example, in a case response the root issue is "current marketing strategy is inappropriate." This is not in the case question, but evidence in the case supports it: e.g., the once successful central purchasing and warehousing approach is more expensive than what competitors use.

Whenever students mention issues and root issues, they get rewarded with marks. Their issues and root issues may reflect a causal relationship. Nevertheless, the mechanical markers seek to reward marks against the most appropriate categories in the guide, and sometimes generously.

Besides issues, analysis, and recommendations, there are marks for format and professionalism. Such rewards should be kept in mind when writing the case response, as a little time devoted to format may pay handsomely. For example, precede the case response with a memorandum. This should be from the person that the student is role playing, to the person and position to whom the case suggests the student is to report. The memorandum should contain a short paragraph linking the case question required with the attached report. The report itself should have headings, e.g., introduction, issues, analysis, recommendations, and conclusion. When using point form, introduce the point with a sentence. There should be a logical flow to the report. And there should be no glaring deficiencies with grammar, spelling, and sentence structure.

Subjective Marking

This method of marking starts with a ranking of the most important issues that need to be addressed. Then, each issue receives a point score consistent with the ranking.

EXHIBIT 3.3
A Sample Marking Guide

Marking Guide for PC Sales Division

Case Approach (1 mark)

* format
* spelling
* grammar
* sentence structure

Issues (3 marks)
(Did the student understand the case? root issues?)

* The sales manager does not have information on the activities of the sales representatives
* The sales manager does not know why the sales representatives are not successful

Analyses (3 marks)
(Did the student understand how the apparent issues were related to the root issues?)

* The sales manager does know which steps work.
* The sales manager does know which steps do not work.
* The sales representatives do not know what is working.
* The sales manager does not know what the customer satisfaction is regarding various steps.

Recommendations (3 marks)
(Did the student understand that the recommendations were to resolve the root issues and the apparent issues?)

* Develop an information system that tracks the sales representatives' adherence to the five steps.

For each issue, a single student score would be awarded based on the identification of the issue and related issues, analysis, and recommendations for resolution. Other factors, such as professionalism and realism, can be scored also.

Subjective marking places more emphasis on the subjective judgment of the marker. It usually takes a few dozen papers before marking consistency can be established. The use of two markers is recommended to reduce bias. This can be waved in favour of time savings when the marker has substantial experience with the case or the case is uncomplicated.

The marking guide for the prior section's PC Sales Division is shown in Exhibit 3.3. Note that there are two stages to the marking. For the issues, analyses, and recommendations, there is a question for each on the overall understanding of the student being marked. For example, for issues, the question is, did the student understand the case? the root issues? These questions provide a means of marking the case response with a subjective assessment on the student's success with responding to the Required in the case question. The points underneath Issues, Analyses, and Recommendations are means of keeping track of how well the student responds to, for example, the analyses.

Case Writing Tactics

The method of marking should not affect how a student responds to a case question. Mechanical marking might favour students using a "shotgun" approach of putting every possible thing down on the case response. Such an approach usually leads to duplication and not much depth or linkage among the various facets of a case question. It would be a poor examination tactic, as it takes time away from a thorough and systematic approach to the case question. Given the time constraints, students should seek to manage their time by understanding the root issues vis-à-vis the "required". They should emphasize identifying, analyzing, and resolving those root issues and, only when time is available, discuss the more tangential issues.

Subjective marking might favour short, uniquely insightful responses. A well-designed mechanical marking guide should do the same. Seeking short, uniquely insightful responses could be dangerous as such responses usually take substantial sifting through the data to find one that addresses all apparent issues, or at least all root issues. It usually takes less time to address issues individually than in total.

A case response that will yield a passing mark must show depth of analysis. This requires sufficient time spent reading the case question in order to understand the case and its issues. The student then has the evidence pointing to the root issues and can undertake the analysis and make appropriate recommendations. If insufficient time is spent reading, the student will have a superficial response and not be able to say much about the issues or to recommend solutions. In a timed situation, however, spending too much time reading leaves insufficient time for responding. Consequently, students should set in advance the length of their reading time and stick to it. To be able to do this, a student needs to understand a variety of possible cases and have a rule for each type. Students should develop their rules that satisfy their own approaches. Two extreme examples follow.

1. For multi-technique cases, 40 percent of the time could be spent reading and 60 percent spent writing. While reading, the relationships between issues and root issues, analysis, and recommendations emerge. Writing time includes time to refine understanding. More ideas will emerge during the writing stage.

2. For a quantitative, directed case like Precious Metals — Case 29 of this casebook — the reading time might fall to about 15 percent, or even less, as the root issues are blatant.

For the majority of student case responses, the earned marks will be the same under both mechanical and subjective marking.

REFERENCES

Ballantine, J.A., and P. McCourt Larres. 2004. "A critical analysis of students' perception of the usefulness of the case study method in an advanced management accounting module: the impact of relevant work experience". *Accounting Education: an international journal* 13(2): 171–189.

Bamber, M., and L. Bamber. 2006. "Using 10-K reports brings management accounting to life". *Issues in Accounting Education* 21(3): 267–290.

Blocher, E.J. 2009. "Teaching cost management: A strategic emphasis". *Issues in Accounting Education* 24(1): 1–12.

Bloom, B.S., M.D. Englehart, G.J. Furst, W.H. Hill, and D.R. Krathwohl. 1956. *Taxonomy of Educational Objectives: The Classification of Educational Goals*. New York: David McKay.

Bonner, S.E. 1999. "Choosing teaching methods based on learning objectives: an integrative framework". *Issues in Accounting Education* 14(1): 11–39.

Christensen, C.M., and P.R. Carlile. 2009. "Course research: using the case method to build and teach management theory". *Academy of Management Learning & Education* 8(2): 240–251.

Clevenger, T.B. 1990. "The Cognitive Domain of Educational Objectives: A Model for Future Accounting Education". Paper presented to the American Accounting Association, annual meeting, Toronto.

Gobeil, J., and F. Phillips. 2001, "Relating case presentation style and level of student knowledge to fact acquisition and application in accounting case analysis". *Issues in Accounting Education* 16(2): 205–222.

Greenhalgh, A.M. 2007. "Case method teaching as a science and art: a metaphoric approach and curricular application". *Journal of Management Education* 31(2): 181–194.

Horngren, C.T., S.M. Datar, G. Foster, M. Rajan, and C. Ittner. 2009. *Cost Accounting: A Managerial Emphasis*, 13th Edition. Upper Saddle River, N.J.: Prentice Hall.

Horngren, C.T., S.M. Datar, G. Foster, M. Rajan, C. Ittner, M.P. Gowing, and S. Janz. 2013. *Cost Accounting: A Managerial Emphasis*, 6th Canadian Edition. Toronto: Pearson.

Johnson, H.T., and R.E. Kaplan. 1987. *Relevance Lost: The Rise and Fall of Management Accounting*. Boston: Harvard Business School Press.

Mauffette-Leenders, L.A., J.A. Erskine, and M.R. Leenders. 1997. *Learning with Cases*. London, Ontario: Richard Ivey School of Business.

Schoenfeld, A.H. 1985. *Mathematical Problem Solving*. San Diego: Academic Press.

Spraakman, G., and B. Jackling. 2014. "A conceptual framework for learning management accounting". *Accounting Perspectives* 13(1): 61–81.

Wynn-Williams, K., R.H. Whiting, and R.W. Adler. 2008. "The influence of business case studies and learning styles: an empirical investigation". *Accounting Education; an international journal* 17(2): 113–128.

SECTION II

Management Accounting Cases

Atcom Manufacturing

Atcom is an international firm that specializes in the manufacture of telecommunication equipment. It was the manufacturing subsidiary and major supplier to a provincial telephone utility. With its early success, Atcom started to sell to customers other than its parent. Then, as part of a privatization policy, the provincial government issued 40 percent of Atcom's common shares to the citizens of the province.

Subsequently, Atcom expanded to a national and, more recently, an international (with one plant in the United States) sales and manufacturing organization. Two years ago, under pressure from customers and potential customers, the parent sold all but 10 percent of its shares. That divestment became part of a strategic plan that emphasized an increased level of new product introduction, especially with respect to computer and electronic technologies.

Within the last year, this accelerated introduction of new products has led to problems with the firm's standard cost system. To explain these problems, it is necessary to understand the various controls that are in place at Atcom. Atcom adopted its parent's control system, with few changes. Thus, Atcom updates its long-range (10-year) plan every two years. Quarterly updates supplement the annual budget and monthly reports against the original budget. Plans and budgets emphasize accountability, and they are done at all levels designated as profit, revenue, or cost centres. The MIS department prepares reports on non-financial information, e.g., capacity utilization, product quality, customer satisfaction. Sales forecasts are the basis of the budgets, and standards are the basis for production costs.

With this overlay of planning, budgeting, and management information systems, every unit of the organization is subject to standard operating activities, an inheritance from the utility parent. Documented activities specify exactly how employees are to undertake their responsibilities. With each unit an experienced staff (who reports to the president) develops the standards. The detailed operating activities specify the steps that employees must perform, the parts and materials to be used, etc. In this way, operating activities provide the basis for evaluating employee performance.

The problem with the standard costs is a result of the rapid rate of new product introduction. The eventually established operating activities are often different and inconsistent with costs committed for new products. Consequently, standard costs may be impossible to meet, or they could be insufficiently demanding. Employees are

29

uncertain about the reasonableness of committed costs, and often there is a lack of motivation to achieve perceived unfair standards.

The president hired you to provide advice on how to resolve the standard cost problem and to get commitment to the budgets and timetable for new products. Within the first few days, you realize that there are two opinions. Among the manufacturing employees, particularly the supervisors, the consensus is that they want to develop detailed activities (i.e., standard operating procedures) before committing to standard costs. They recognize and welcome the expectation that there will be a learning curve and lower unit costs as production volumes increase. However, they insist upon a factual starting point consisting of activities by accountable employees.

The other consensus comes from the marketing employees. They say the production cost standards cannot wait for the detailed activities that determine the standard costs. They admit to the thoroughness and reduced risk from activities-based standard costs. They insist, however, that taking the time to establish the detailed activities will delay the introduction schedule for each new product by between six months and one year, and delay has already caused problems for them. To resolve the conflict they suggest that standard costs should be determined by expected results, from which several different sets of activities could then be selected. Some marketing people are even questioning the need for standard costs. They cite, as evidence in favour of eliminating standard costs, just-in-time inventory systems, the large proportion of purchased components, and the declining share of costs going to direct labour.

Required

The president has asked you to implement a solution for introducing new products without delay or lack of control. You are to use the case approach.

Bert The Baker

You are a management accountant with the divisional accounting office of a large grocery retailer, Eastons. Your supervisor has asked you to go to the Richville store to resolve an issue between the store manager and the bakery manager about the fairness of the accounting information used for a bonus system.

In order to remain viable and to grow, Eastons introduced sales and profit targets for its retail stores. For an "A-type" store like the Richville store, the weekly sales target is $12 per square foot; or, for this 20,000 square-foot store, $12.5 million a year. Operating profits are to be 5 percent of target sales, or $625,000 a year.

Typically, store managers delegate responsibility for sales and operating profits to department managers, i.e., produce, dry goods, bakery, and meats. With this system, the store managers and their department managers receive bonuses equal to about one third of their salaries if the targets are achieved.

Upon arriving at the Richville store, you meet Stella, the store manager, and then Bert, the baker. Bert reiterates his complaint that the bonus system is based on unfair accounting.

> I am told that my sales target is $1.75 million a year, or about $33,655 a week. I have no problem with sales. I can provide customers with what they want at competitive prices. However, I have a problem with my annual profit target of $150,000, which is 8.5 percent of sales. My complaint has nothing to do with the 8.5 percent profit target being more than the 5 percent for the overall store. A bakery has a better chance of high profits than the other departments.

> Let me explain. First, I have little control over my labour costs. The store manager schedules employees who may or may not be necessary for the bakery. Second, the bakery operating statement includes charges that have nothing to do with the bakery. For example, the store manager's total salary is charged to the bakery because it is always profitable. Third, I do not get the chance to approve any of the costs charged to the bakery department. Fourth, I do not receive a copy of the bakery operating statement. Fifth, and most important, there is no

31

opportunity to plan the operating costs in conjunction with the store manager and the other department managers. This would allow costs to be managed more carefully.

Required

As the management accountant, you are to use the case approach to identify and analyze the issues and make recommendations for their resolution.

Binson's Country Markets

Binson's was established as a fruit and vegetable business vendor in 1929, when Arthur (age 18) and Robert Binson (age 16) began delivering produce from a truck in Toronto. They were joined by their brothers, Jack and Gordon, and their father Fred. In 1939 they moved their business to a store at 1114 St. Clair Avenue in Toronto, which was called Binson's Fruit Market. At that time, all four brothers and their father Fred worked in the store. Ruby, Ethel, Doris, Gwen, Mary and Ruth assisted in the store, making it a true family business. During the war years, Art and Jack stayed home to keep the business going while Bob and Gord served with the army. Following the war, the brothers again delivered their produce in the west end of Toronto, this time in a large bus that was converted into a store on wheels. The name, Binson's, was placed on the front of the bus.

In 1956 Gord and his family purchased the existing property in Newmarket, which is north of Toronto. The original Newmarket store was operational from the May 24th weekend until Thanksgiving each year to sell local fruit and vegetables to travellers. Customers, largely from Toronto, were travelling north each Friday to their cottages and returning on Sunday. In 1967 a grandson, John, was made manager; he immediately kept the store opened 12 months a year, which was possible with the steady customer flow caused by the population growth of Newmarket and surrounding towns and the steady supply of fruit and vegetables from the United States and other spots in the south. Another grandson, Ray, joined the business in 1975, and they started a second store in a nearby community, Aurora. The two grandsons had outstanding success in expanding the product lines and customer base at the two stores. Most important was the brand image of Binson's for fresh, high quality products.

John and Ray died late last year in a car accident. You have just acquired the business from their estates. With the strong brand recognition of Binson's Country Markets, you are planning to expand the number of stores into a chain in Ontario and elsewhere in Canada and North America.

You quickly learn that the two present stores were run effectively and efficiently by John and Ray, who were non-traditional but outstanding managers. John managed the Newmarket store (with about 100 employees) and looked after all ordering and merchandising. Ray managed the Aurora Store (with about 80 employees), as well as all advertisement and promotion. They co-operated fully and worked long hours. They directed all employees in their respective stores with firm but gentle hands. There were no other managers or supervisors, and there were no written procedures or reports. Annually, a local chartered accountant prepared the financial statements for statutory and income tax reasons.

With the help of two long-time employees you have run the two stores for the last three months. One of these employees worked in the Newmarket deli, while the other worked with produce in the Aurora store. Although both were hardworking and dedicated employees, neither of them had had any supervisory experience. Consequently, the employee scheduling was not being done carefully. The employees basically scheduled themselves. The result was that during the busy periods when customers shopped (Thursday and Friday nights and Saturday and Sunday during the day), there were very few employees. Employees made themselves available during week days, when the customers were less plentiful.

You admit that you have not had the time to properly schedule employees to departments or to ensure an adequate level of customer service without excessive costs. In hindsight, there has been excess staffing at times, and inadequate staffing at other times.

As there was only one income statement prepared after the year end (Exhibit 1), you were unclear as to the profitability of each store. Similarly, you were unclear of the profitability of each department in each store, other than the sales by department, which are captured by the cash registers (Exhibit 2).

You realize that a professional general manager will need to be hired for each store. These two managers will report directly to you, along with a project team for expanding the number of stores, a controller, and a director of advertisement and promotion. From an examination of the sales by department for each store, you estimate that six supervisors might be needed at each store. Each supervisor will need to be responsible for one or more sales departments.

In considering the assignment of departments to supervisors, the following appears to be a preliminary arrangement:

- Bakery, fresh breads
- Bulk foods, groceries
- Dairy, frozen foods
- Deli meats, cheese, olive bar, salad bar, prepared foods, delivery, e-mail sales
- Meat, poultry, fish
- Produce (fruit and vegetables), flowers

You recognize that for the future well-being of the stores, non-financial measures are necessary. However, as a first step you want to establish a management accounting system that will ensure profitability of departments and stores with return on sales and return on investment. You want to use the new system for the two existing stores as well all new stores.

You have been considering the installation of new loading docks at the Newmarket and the Aurora stores. The new dock will speed up unloading, thereby getting the goods on the shelves more quickly. The new equipment will cost $300,000, and it will have a life of 10 years with a salvage value of $50,000. The vendor will finance 90 percent of the value at six percent per year. As more goods will be on the shelves sooner and longer, you expect sales to increase by $100,000 per year. The main advantage will be that the new equipment will save $50,000 annually in labour costs. The cost of capital is eight percent, and the tax shield equals

Exhibit 1
Net Income Statement, Last Year ($ 000s)

Sales		$31,838
Cost of goods sold		
Opening inventory	4,943	
Purchases	21,603	
Ending inventory	(4,259)	22,287
General and administrative expenses		
Employee salaries, wages, benefits	1,552	
Rent	1,184	
Amortization (non vehicle)	543	
Utilities	458	
Materials and supplies	720	
Vehicle expenses	722	
Advertisement and promotion	1,865	
Other expenses	167	7,211
Net income before income taxes		$ 2,340

Exhibit 2
Sales Breakdown by Store, Last Year ($ 000s)

Department	Newmarket	Aurora
Bakery, fresh breads	$ 3,766	$ 2,866
Bulk foods	643	569
Dairy	571	450
Deli meats and cheeses	4,940	3,276
Delivery, e-mail sales	747	627
Flowers	465	324
Frozen foods	737	657
Groceries	1,849	701
Meat, poultry, fish	2,495	2,569
Olive bar, salad bar	948	877
Prepared foods	518	484
Produce (fruit and vegetables)	449	311
Total	$18,128	$13,711

$$\text{Tax Shield Rate} = \frac{T \times C}{C + R} \times \frac{2 + R}{2(1 + R)}$$

where
T = the income tax rate, 30 percent
C = the CCA rate, 30 percent
R = the cost of capital or required rate of return, eight percent.

Required
Use the case approach to specify the management accounting requirements and to assess the proposal for new loading docks.

CASE 4

Brights Lodging and Travel

Some owners of hotel properties have been establishing new medium-priced, good quality hotels in dilapidated downtown locations. The new properties are either new buildings built on vacant land or major renovations to existing buildings, previously used for other purposes. There are two reasons for placing new hotels into seedy downtown areas where the neighbours might include ramshackle rows of shops, night-clubs with bulletproof glass, and homeless people. First, there is the strategy of devel-oping up-and-coming locations in major U.S. cities, and thereby taking advantage of the expected return of people to inner cities. These properties are a bet on urban renewals and increased property values. Second, these downtown hotels provide convenient accommodations for busy business travellers who want good quality without paying for unnecessary opulence. They also have a wager on a change in business practices from opulence to basic quality, saving travellers money and increasing the returns to hotels.

There is a simple but consistent format for each hotel chain participating in these urban renewals. For one major chain the rooms surround a central pool, there is plenty of parking for rental cars, all rooms have functional desks and data ports for laptops, and the modest lobbies have breakfast buffets. Their uniformity makes these urban renewals easy to spot, and thereby reduces the need for adver-tisement.

A new building on vacant land does not pose any significant problems. Renovating existing alternative use buildings can have problems, and these renovations may be 20 to 30 percent more expensive than comparable new buildings. Renovations may be fur-ther complicated. Antiquated plumbing and electrical systems often are more expensive to rebuild than to replace with new systems. Older buildings have layouts that pose challenges. One renovation example is where two king-size beds fit in room 801 but not into 701. The problem is that the building's walls are inches thicker at the base, making the lower-floor rooms smaller. Nevertheless, renovations are often required to meet specific municipal regulations.

During the past year, Brights Lodging and Travel Corporation (BLT) has managed 26 of these urban renewal hotels, and it has signed an agreement to manage another six for another hotel chain starting next year. It should be noted that there are often two players in the delivery of hotel services. First, there are the owners of the hotel buildings, such as those developing no-frills urban renewals. Second, there are the management companies, such as BLT, that manage the hotels. The latter hire all employees, buy all supplies and food, and maintain all equipment and facilities. These management firms work on the basis of a share of the top-line revenue or a share in the profits.

As the management accountant at BLT, you have been asked by the board of directors and the CEO (who is a member of the board and a major shareholder of BLT) to develop a balanced scorecard. She recently attended a hotel management conference where there was a session on the benefits from using the balanced scorecard. To advise you, the CEO has formed a committee consisting of herself, the controller, two owner representatives, and three general managers from successful BLT-managed hotels.

The committee established a series of meetings to exchange information for guiding you with the balanced scorecard. In the end, they provided you with advice on all four perspectives of the balanced scorecard.

Financial Perspective

The committee noted that financial measures have been the basis for gauging the effectiveness of hotel management, despite other factors — such as customer satisfaction and employee (associate) turnover — having a direct effect on financial performance. BLT uses Navision to produce operating statements for each hotel and chain, with the format shown in Exhibit 1. The hotel example in the exhibit has 297 rooms for rent 365 days a year, and an annual occupancy rate of 80 percent for the most recent year. (Occupancy is the number of rooms occupied divided by the total rooms available.) This occupancy level is above average but not exceptional. Ninety percent of the revenues come from room rentals. There are four classes of expenses: cost of goods sold, payroll, controllable, and uncontrollable.

BLT monitors performances at the property (i.e., hotel) and corporate (all properties managed for a chain) levels to ensure that the owners' long-term objectives are being met. Presently, BLT manages a portfolio of 26 hotels with annual sales of $278 million. This sales volume represents substantial growth during the last decade, when the company started with twelve hotels and $63 million in annual revenues. BLT's board of directors, consisting of all shareholders of BLT, wants sales to grow at the rate of 15 percent per year for the next decade with hotel profitability maintained at the current levels. The board also wants BLT-managed hotels to outperform competitors. Although BLT-managed hotels are doing well, they are not meeting the expectation of the board:

- they are *not* in the top 20 percent in guest scores and profitability;
- the turnover rate of hourly employees is *not* less than 60 percent annually;
- the turnover rate of managers is *not* less than 20 percent annually;
- budgets are *not* always achieved; and
- owners' unlevered returns on investment are *not* always equal to or greater than 15 percent.

More specifically, the BLT committee agreed on two financial measures for the balanced scorecard. The first indicator was a yield index that gauges a property's revenue per available room (RevPAR) relative to competitive hotels as well as to year-over-year improvement. The inherent objective is to achieve both higher RevPAR levels and faster RevPAR growth rates than those of competitors. The second indicator is an index of operating performance relative to a flexible budget. Rather than

Exhibit 1
Operating Statement

	Latest Year
Rooms available	108,405
Rooms occupied	86,714
Average rate	82.79
Revenue	
Rooms	$7,179,052
Food	306,198
Beverage	51,203
Telephone	289,890
Other	138,468
Total	7,964,811
Cost of goods sold	
Telephone	42,257
Telephone equipment	22,893
Other	311,001
Total cost of goods	376,151
Payroll	
Housekeeping	466,472
Laundry	53,987
Front desk	122,550
Administration	86,123
Sales	27,024
Maintenance	82,286
Management (salary)	279,335
Employee relations	25,670
Other	121,455
Total payroll	1,264,902
Controllable expenses	
Linen and laundry	46,826
Guest supplies	70,983
Cleaning expense	44,867
Rooms, other	92,022
Postage	9,750
Office supplies	20,748
Administration telephone	19,032
Travel	15,459
Cashier (overage) or shortage	364
Bad debt expense	7,965
Administration, other	35,274
Advertising	21,840
Maintenance supplies	9,165
Maintenance trash	29,303
Maintenance	99,489
Utilities	275,360
House charges, other	49,686
Total controllable expenses	848,133
Total operating expenses	2,489,186
Contribution to profits	5,475,625
Uncontrollable expenses	1,590,392
House profit	$3,885,233

focusing on property-profit achievement relative to budget, the committee designed this index, which is part of the operating statement in Exhibit 1, to consider only expenses that are controllable by hotel general managers and, simultaneously, adjust expected performance to account for variances in business volume (occupancy). The committee called this a flow-through model, and with it they expected the following:

- meet budget targets,
- demonstrate superior financial management of hotels,
- outperform competitors in profitability and expense-control,
- achieve internal consistency in property operations, and
- deliver high investment returns to owners.

The committee was particularly pleased with the flow-through model's ability to re-forecast controllable costs using a fixed and variable cost model to adjust performance expectations to reflect actual room rentals. Line items that vary with respect to occupancy are re-forecasted every period that actual occupancy differs from budgeted occupancy. The result is a line item entitled, "Contribution to house profit from controllable items." This line item incorporates expenditures over which the general manager has considerable control, e.g., payroll, utilities, maintenance, office supplies. However, it does not include items over which the general manager has little or no control, e.g., franchise fees, health and welfare insurance, travel-agent commissions. The advantage of excluding uncontrollable items is that general managers can be held to a higher level of accountability for items that they control without facing the frustration of unanticipated changes to uncontrollable items.

An additional benefit of the flow-through model as a management tool is that it allows owners to focus on management and cost control issues that might otherwise be buried within the financial operating statement. Those factors are exposed in the variance calculations for each line item that is under management control.

The committee recognized that measuring operating performance strictly on financial measures is inconsistent with the long-term investment horizon and with BLT's corporate objectives. Furthermore, they repeatedly noted that financial measures are lagging indicators rather than leading indicators and cannot be used to predict future performance. BLT needs, according to the committee, measures that track financial results while simultaneously monitoring progress in building the capability and acquiring the intangible assets needed for future growth. The committee agreed that the balanced scorecard must have the following characteristics:

- not limited to financial performance;
- nonfinancial performance measures dealing with factors important for long-term growth and value creation;
- inclusion of factors that lead to growth, profitability, and physical maintenance;
- simple to monitor; and
- easy for general managers to understand and accept.

Customer Perspective

The committee reviewed the following potential guest-related indicators: customer satisfaction, customer retention, new-customer acquisition, market segmentation, market share, customer profitability, responsiveness, associate knowledge and service levels, and mystery-guest assessments.

Exhibit 2
Outline of BLT Consolidated Process Audit

Human-resources best practices

1. Personnel files are properly maintained, e.g., reviews, discipline, tax forms
2. Associates adhere to training schedules
3. Uniforms are worn per policy
4. Hotel complies with provincial and federal human resources regulations

Hotel-improvement best practices

1. Associates are aware of mission statement, critical success factors
2. Guest rooms and public areas are properly cleaned and inspected
3. Defects and guest complaints are properly recorded and resolved
4. Sales and marketing goals are posted and results tracked properly
5. Hotel adheres to accounting and internal-control processes

Maintenance best practices

1. Guest rooms and public areas are refreshed with quarterly preventive maintenance
2. Major equipment items are maintained according to schedule
3. Inspections are kept current, e.g., fire, elevator, health
4. Pool readings are conducted and logged correctly
5. Capital-expenditure file is maintained correctly

Internal research found that guest scores correlate with investment returns, thus substantiating the value to owners of high guest-satisfaction levels. Properties that scored in the top 20 percent of guest-satisfaction scores provided investment returns averaging 17.4 percent in the most recent year. Properties that scored in the top 40 percent of the guest-satisfaction scores still managed a 15.2 percent, while properties below median levels provided only a 12.7 percent return.

Internal Business Processes

The committee evaluated a number of internal business process measures that might bear on the objectives of both management and owners, including the following: associate-productivity rates, service errors and failure rates, maintenance of physical assets, capital-expenditure efficiency, accounting and internal-control practices, and time required to complete key processes and tasks, e.g., check-in, maintenance, breakfast seating, and serving.

BLT predominantly manages national franchise affiliations; thus, general managers have only minimal control over the matters relating to marketing and brand recognition. Furthermore, a number of the indicators dealing with efficiency and productivity rates are indirectly reflected in the financial flow-through model. The committee developed a comprehensive hotel audit program to check and verify that general managers comply with the internal business process expectations or standards. These criteria are shown in Exhibit 2. Each audit is to be conducted by a manager of internal audit against a detailed check list of items. If there is compliance to all items, the hotel (i.e., its general manager) receives a perfect control of 100 points. Hotels receiving less than 90 points are expected to have serious operating shortcomings. Only with more than 97.5 points will general managers be excused from remedial actions.

Learning and Growth

The committee considered the following possible measures to gauge the learning and growth:

- personal growth of associates (employees);
- internal promotion levels;
- associate satisfaction;
- associate retention;
- associate empowerment;
- strategic skills of associates, managers, and the organization; training levels and cycle times;
- cross-training levels of associates and line manager;
- information technology use;
- access to strategic information;
- new initiatives explored or implemented; and
- community participation and knowledge exhibited by general managers.

With a median associate turnover rate of 88.3 percent, BLT experienced many personnel issues common to the hospitality industry. That level of turnover meant the company was constantly replacing workers, spending time and energy on training, and experiencing reduced guest-satisfaction levels because of mistakes made by inexperienced associates. Thus, associate (employee) retention presented the greatest opportunity for improvement within the organization. Furthermore, the committee determined that many of the other measures, although valid, would be ineffective in the absence of a stable base of long-term associates. A supplemental analysis showed that hotels with associate turnover below 100 percent (which is still substantial) enjoyed generally higher profit and RevPAR growth than those with turnover levels exceeding 100 percent. Given the negative impact of associate turnover, the committee recommended that the balanced scorecard emphasize the reduction in turnover levels.

Required

As the management accountant and a member of the balanced scorecard committee, use the case approach to complete the balanced scorecard for BLT.

CASE 5

CCP Publishers

You have been hired by Chris Paraskevopoulos, who is an economics professor emeritus at your university. After retiring from teaching, Chris started an academic publishing business, which publishes university textbooks and trade books, the latter being academic books written by university professors for academic and professional audiences.

CCP Publishers is located on the 10th floor of a building in the northern part of the city. It also leases 500 square metres in the basement of the building for its warehouse operations. Chris is the chief editor as well as the CEO. There are four editors in addition to Chris, three editorial assistants, four marketing representatives, a business manager (yourself), and a warehouse supervisor. Chris and the four editors are all equal partners. The marketing representatives are responsible for selling CCP books to university and commercial bookstores.

The business model has changed little since CCP was established three years ago. Authors either contact an editor, or the editor contacts the author. In either situation, when there is an agreement between the author (or authors) and an editor that the book will be economically viable, a contract is signed that specifies the general content of the book, a publication schedule, and responsibilities for both CCP and the author or authors. An editor from CCP works with each author (or author group) in the development of a book. Currently, 35 books are in various stages of production. CCP has 42 books in print and available for sale. Most activities are contracted out, including copyediting, layout, index development, art work, photography, and printing. After printing, books are shipped directly to university and commercial bookstores.

The income statement for the latest fiscal year is shown below:

Sales	$ 975,000
Cost of books sold	(210,000)
Salaries and wages	(540,000)
Rental	(87,000)
Shipping	(62,000)
Miscellaneous	(52,000)
Operating income	$ 24,000

Chris has some concerns about the profitability of CCP. He believes that CCP should be more profitable. He would like to control the development costs for book. He would also like to know the profitability of each book, and how that profitability compares with expectations of the editor when the contract is signed. Consequently, you were hired as the business manager.

Required

As the business manager, use the case approach to address the CEO's profitability concerns.

CASE 6

Clearwater Small Appliances

Clearwater manufactures a wide range of small household appliances, such as coffee makers, can openers, microwave and toaster ovens, irons and ironing boards. In 50 years of existence, it has prospered and established a well-respected brand name. Business has been good — at least up to now. Recent changes in methods of retailing require Clearwater to alter significantly its way of doing business. Traditionally, Clearwater has supplied retailers such as department stores, hardware stores, and discount stores. They now are suffering declining sales because giant category retailers like Home Depot, Canadian Tire, and Wal-Mart dominate the market. These "power retailers" use sophisticated information and inventory management. Their finely tuned selections and competitive pricing crowd out weaker retailers. The forecast is that category retailers will continue gaining market share.

So powerful have category retailers become that they tell even the largest and most powerful manufacturers what goods to make, in what colours and sizes, and how much to ship and when. In fact, they dictate practically all terms of business with their suppliers. Some category retailers even charge the manufacturers for shipment errors. They constantly squeeze costs; for example, some have operating and selling expenses as low as 15 percent of sales, compared to 28 percent for traditional department stores. The difference is even greater than these 13 percentage points, as the sales prices are about 5 percent lower for the category retailers than for department stores.

In order to survive, Clearwater must supply category stores; to be a supplier, Clearwater must tailor its products to please individual category retailers and meet high standards for on time, defect-free merchandise. However, Clearwater wants to preserve its brand name "Clearwater" instead of merely manufacturing store brands. Supplying category retailers is, for Clearwater, only a coping strategy. It recognizes that it needs to supply the category retailers, but it also recognizes that to survive, Clearwater must have a separate and strong identity.

The management team developed a new strategy. In formulating it, they sought substantial input from all parts of Clearwater. As well, buyers and executives from three of the largest category retailers provided insights about what changes would be required to meet their needs. The result is the following internal statement, endorsed by the board of directors.

Tactics for Coping With Category Retailers

Protect our brands. If customers ask for our products by name, the category retailers are more likely to stock our products. Consequently, we must advertise, and not merely depend on the category retailers for exposure.

- **Customize.** Meet customer requirements — whether directed by category retailer or inferred by customer.

- **Innovate constantly.** Non-distinguishable products are vulnerable because category retailers can readily replace suppliers or contract for the manufacture of their own brands.

- **Organize around the category retailer.** The organization will reorganize into multi-disciplinary teams, each of which will serve the largest category retailers.

- **Invest in technology.** The category retailers demand the latest information technology to ensure that the right products arrive on the shelves at the right time.

- **Cut the fat.** If we do not constantly reduce our costs and pass the savings on to the category retailers, they will find manufacturers that can and do.

You, as the vice-president controller, with the management team, have been fully involved in formulating the strategy by which to become a profitable supplier to category retailers. You are now to develop an information system for planning (i.e., budgeting one to three years into the future) and monitoring the strategy. This information is to be incorporated into the monthly cost of quality report, which you are also to review and make changes to in order to improve its functionality, as necessary.

Cost of Quality Report

Prevention
- Quality engineering
- Receiving inspection
- Quality training

Appraisal
- Product inspection

Internal Failures
- Scrap
- Rework

External Failures
- Net cost of returned products

The cost of quality report is compiled monthly by the production vice-president and one of the production scheduling engineers, using estimates based on his experience. Separate tracking and budgeting do not occur for these costs. The production vice-president is responsible for quality, but many of her subordinates are in better positions for ensuring it.

Required

Undertake your project using the case approach and report your findings to the management committee.

Coffee Maker Supreme

Coffee Maker Supreme (CMS) has been in the business of manufacturing coffee makers for three generations. During the first and second generations the growth in demand was modestly positive, and customers seemed to have been more content with product range and quality. During the time of the present generation of owners, the demand for coffee machines grew at a much higher rate. That demand does not appear to be declining in the foreseeable future. Moreover, customers have become increasingly demanding of specialized and high-quality coffee makers.

CMS is a privately owned manufacturer and distributor of machines to make coffee. Sales are more than $200 million per year. Customers — from all parts of the world — are restaurants, cafes, and cafeterias. Sales are made by commissioned sales representatives supported by a website to process orders and to provide after-sales service. CMS started in the Canadian market, but expanded into the United States a decade before the free-trade agreement. Nicole Roberto joined the business after completing her accounting designation. Two years earlier, she had completed her undergraduate degree in business. She encouraged her father to purchase coffee machine manufacturers in France and Italy in order to expand into the European market. She then spent a decade in Europe developing the business. Her heritage language — Italian — and her French immersion studies from grades 1 to 12 assisted her in successfully developing the European business.

In year T_{-5}, the sales representatives from around the world were provided with Web-based sales support for transacting sales and for the customers to obtain post-sales service and support. This system proved highly successful, allowing CMS to further expand into Europe and into the Japanese and Mexican markets. The global reach with plants in Canada, the United States, France and Italy meant that there was a rather haphazard product line. The four plants produced 27 products, of which 10 were literally duplicates of another 10, resulting in only 17 truly different products. In 2010, the product line was rationalized, allowing two of the plants to be closed and for the product line to be increased by 13 new coffee makers that were different from existing products. Of the current 30 different coffee makers, 16 are manufactured in one plant, and 14 are manufactured in the other. In effect, the new products expanded both ends of the product line — i.e., both larger-capacity and small, special-purpose coffee makers. Moreover, features were added to make all coffee makers more versatile. In effect, each of the 30 products experienced product design and manufacturing process changes.

Global sourcing was introduced at the same time to ensure procurement of the most appropriate and cost-effective materials and components. Along with global sourcing, the decades-old practice of 100 percent inspection was replaced with a more modern system of random checks. This allowed for most of the inspectors to be reassigned. Suppliers were responsible for quality of all materials and components, and manufacturing workers were responsible for quality control in the manufacturing process. Each worker knew the operating specifications, and if a unit received at his or her station was not up to standard, the manufacturing process could be stopped for the necessary corrections.

The financial results of the first full year of operations with the product line and related changes are shown in Exhibit 1. These results were what president Nicole Roberto showed you as you started your first day as the controller. Nicole had been brought back to Canada three months earlier, when the previous president had been obliged to retire for health reasons.

The first task assigned to you by Nicole was to determine why, when sales targets were met, operating income was substantially lower than budget. You first reviewed the variance. The sales variance at one percent was trivial. After talking to the manufacturing vice-president, who was in charge of both plants, you concluded that the material variance is largely attributable to some yield problems with some materials and components and that these yield problems created the unfavourable variances for direct labour and variable manufacturing overhead. A bigger problem was the fixed manufacturing overhead. The manufacturing vice-president explained this variance to be the result of charging to fixed manufacturing overhead, the rework required in getting the plants accustomed to manufacturing the new and newly designed products.

Exhibit 1

Operating Statement, Year T ($000,000s)

	Budget	Actual	Variance
Sales	$216.0	$218.3	$ 2.3
Cost of Goods Sold			
Variable costs:			
Materials	62.7	64.8	(2.1)
Manufacturing labour	10.6	11.4	(0.8)
Manufacturing overhead	23.7	25.1	(1.4)
Selling	8.6	8.7	(0.1)
	105.6	110.0	(4.4)
Contribution Margin	110.4	108.3	(2.1)
Fixed Expenses			
Manufacturing overhead	49.4	66.1	(16.7)
Selling	10.7	10.6	0.1
Administration	18.6	18.7	(0.1)
	78.7	95.4	(16.7)
Operating Income	$ 31.7	$ 12.9	$(18.8)

Exhibit 2

Cost of Quality Report ($000,000s)

	Years					
	T	T$_{-1}$	T$_{-2}$	T$_{-3}$	T$_{-4}$	T$_{-5}$
Prevention costs	$ 1.2	$3.1	$3.2	$3.0	$2.8	$2.6
Appraisal costs	0.1	1.3	1.4	1.2	1.0	1.0
Internal failure costs	2.1	1.1	1.0	0.7	0.8	0.8
External failure costs	6.7	0.6	0.2	0.6	0.3	0.4
Total quality costs	$10.1	$6.1	$5.8	$5.5	$4.9	$4.8

Exhibit 3

Customer Satisfaction Survey
(December surveys, % score on a 0% to 100% scale)

	Years					
	T	T$_{-1}$	T$_{-2}$	T$_{-3}$	T$_{-4}$	T$_{-5}$
Product quality	61.5	85.5	84.7	85.9	86.1	85.3
Durability	58.3	93.3	92.7	92.2	92.7	93.6
Good value	48.6	75.1	77.5	76.6	78.1	76.4
Features	88.6	53.8	56.3	55.8	54.7	53.1

Warranty work was also charged to fixed manufacturing overhead, whether an actual or estimated charge. You also asked for and received the cost of quality report (Exhibit 2) and the customer satisfaction survey results (Exhibit 3).

Required
As the controller, carry out your assignment using the case approach.

CASE 8

Consolidated Pump

Your firm, Consolidated Pump, is a major manufacturer and distributor of industrial pumps. Due to technological advances in pump design and manufacturing, sales and profits have grown substantially. Other firms, observing this growth, have entered or expanded their presence in the pump market, and consequently competition has intensified. See Exhibits 1 and 2 for the impact of recent competition on financial performance.

Exhibit 1
CONSOLIDATED PUMP
Summary of Financial Statements
($000,000s)

	Years			
	T	T$_{-1}$	T$_{-2}$	T$_{-3}$
Sales	$112	$ 95	$ 81	$ 69
Less:				
Variable manufacturing cost of goods sold	15	18	18	22
Variable marketing and administrative costs	8	7	6	4
Total variable costs	23	25	24	26
Contribution margin	89	70	57	43
Deduct:				
Fixed manufacturing costs	50	34	27	18
Fixed marketing and administrative costs	27	24	20	16
Total fixed costs	77	58	47	34
Operating income	12	12	10	9
Net income after taxes	$ 7	$ 7	$ 6	$ 5
Inventories	$ 29	$ 23	$ 19	$ 10
Total assets	$ 50	$ 48	$ 43	$ 39
Long-term bonds	$ 17	$ 19	$ 23	$ 21
Owners' equity	$ 24	$ 19	$ 12	$ 9

Exhibit 2
Consolidated Pump's Comparative Performance Data
(as a percentage of industry total)

Year	Sales	Net Income	Total Assets	Owners' Equity
T_{-11}	4.7	5.1	4.5	5.2
T_{-10}	4.9	5.3	4.6	5.5
T_{-9}	4.7	5.4	4.7	5.4
T_{-8}	4.8	5.9	4.5	5.9
T_{-7}	4.9	6.0	5.0	5.8
T_{-6}	5.0	6.4	5.1	6.4
T_{-5}	6.0	7.2	6.2	7.0
T_{-4}	6.4	7.1	6.2	7.4
T_{-3}	7.0	8.5	6.8	7.7
T_{-2}	7.2	12.4	7.7	9.5
T_{-1}	8.6	13.1	7.9	10.2
T	9.5	11.4	7.9	10.3

The technological advances have been applicable to a wide range of pumps, and Consolidated Pump has purchased several previously autonomous pump manufacturers that produced related products. Consolidated Pump then improved the technology of its pumps and its manufacturing processes. As a result, Consolidated Pump now produces 87 different products. The number of inventoried parts for making pumps has grown more rapidly than has the number of assembled pumps. Because of the large number of different parts, the purchasing department costs have grown at a particularly rapid rate. This has been a concern, and the business analyst studied these costs. Exhibit 3 shows this analysis.

The standard price equals total cost plus a markup of 80 percent. Product costs equal direct materials, direct labour, and overhead allocated on direct labour hours. In the past, this pricing practice has been satisfactory. Due to near total automation of production, direct labour is now only 9 percent of manufacturing costs. Materials are about 10 percent. The remaining 81 percent comes from manufacturing overhead. Senior management has become suspicious of the allocation of overhead based on direct labour; a detailed study of activities found that time in production was a more valid indicator of the manufacturing overhead consumed by a product than direct labour hours. For this alternative approach to assigning manufacturing overhead, you have gathered the preliminary data contained in Exhibit 4. It is unclear whether there is any value in changing the allocation base.

Parts inventories have been increasing in recent years to where now they are out of control. The annual budget makes provision for a parts inventory based on last year, with adjustments for changes to the product line to be assembled. This approach to inventory planning has led to excesses for some parts and shortages for others. However, the nature of the pump business is that pumps manufactured and shipped represent firm orders. For most pumps, demand is highly predictable, and parts are readily available within one to two days. However, the higher-priced pumps are more difficult to forecast.

Exhibit 3
Analysis of Consolidated Pump's Purchasing Department

Senior management has been concerned that costs have increased at an alarming rate in the purchasing department, although the director of purchasing regularly overworks her purchasing agents. The analysis sought to identify the causes of growth in purchasing department costs and then understand how to control those factors. As a first step, the analyst asked purchasing employees what were the reasons for their activities. Although 11 cost drivers were initially identified, after analysis, the director reasoned that three cost drivers were significant: sales, number of different pumps, and number of different parts.

Multiple regression was initially used on the 12 years of data, but multi-collinearity was greater than 0.8. Below are the results from simple regression for three cost drivers (independent variables) and purchasing department total costs (the dependent variable).

Variable	Coefficient*	Standard Error*
Regression Number 1		
Constant	5,702.1	2,741.3
Independent variable 1:		
Sales in dollars ($r^2 = 0.46$)	1.9	1.2
Regression Number 2		
Constant	2,491.7	1,021.6
Independent variable 1:		
Number of different pumps ($r^2 = 0.32$)	61.4	70.3
Regression Number 3		
Constant	40.4	25.8
Independent variable 1:		
Number of different parts ($r^2 = 0.79$)	5.9	1.6

* Elimination of some zeros for the coefficients and standard errors, did not distort the relationships between respective coefficient and standard error.

Exhibit 4
Allocation of Consolidated Pump's Costs, Product Pricing

The 87 pumps made by Consolidated Pump can be aggregated into five classes. The cost of an individual pump is a variation of its class, reflecting more or fewer materials and processing time. The idea of a class of pump simplifies production and marketing.

	Class				
	A	B	C	D	E
Standard Unit Costs					
Direct Labour	$ 4.22	$ 6.17	$ 7.87	$ 10.48	$ 14.69
Materials	3.40	5.10	6.07	7.92	9.74
Overhead*	31.68	42.24	50.69	71.81	107.71
	$39.30	$53.51	$ 64.63	$ 90.21	$132.14
Consolidated's Standard Price	$70.74	$96.32	$116.33	$162.38	$237.85
Competitors Price	$69.00	$93.00	$114.00	$170.00	$240.00
Units Sold	51,100	52,400	57,400	411,400	127,400
Direct labour hours, actual	1.5	2.0	2.4	3.4	5.1
Time in (hours) production, actual	5.2	7.1	15.0	18.2	26.5

* Manufacturing overhead is allocated to products with the following formula:
$$\frac{\text{Budgeted Overhead in dollars}}{\text{Budgeted Direct Labour in hours}} \times \text{actual direct labour hours}$$

Required

The controller asked you, a management accountant, to use the case approach to (1) identify the reasons for profit problems through quantitative and qualitative analysis, and (2) recommend solutions.

CASE 9

Construction Equipment Manufacturing

Construction Equipment Manufacturing Limited (CEML) is Canada's largest manufacturer of excavating (digging) equipment. It produces five major product lines through 13 manufacturing divisions and sells these products with one sales division. All manufacturing divisions buy and sell extensively among one another. The sales division is a profit centre.

CEML was established in Saskatchewan in the 1920s to build equipment to extract potash (a fertilizer) from underground mines. After 1950 the company expanded into the manufacturing of other mining equipment, especially for coal mining, but also for all other types of mining. In the late 1970s, CEML expanded into making particularly specialized excavation equipment for the oil sands open-pit mining industry of Alberta. Through the acquisitions of other excavation equipment manufacturers, CEML had, by 2000, become the largest manufacturer and seller of excavation equipment in North America.

In 2005 CEML initiated co-branding and supply agreements with several key suppliers, including a leading European manufacturer of excavation equipment. Then, in 2008, CEML obtained a co-branding supply agreement with a Japanese firm to offer excavator solutions to customers in Asian markets. Presently, Saskatchewan-based CEML is the largest manufacturer and distributor of specialized excavation equipment in the world.

Transfer prices among the manufacturing divisions have been set at standard variable cost plus a 40 percent markup to cover other costs and profit. This transfer price system has been satisfactory for decades. However, recently two changes have occurred to make this transfer price unsatisfactory. First, CEML changed its responsibility accounting system. Now all manufacturing divisions are investment centres rather than cost centres, and the general managers of manufacturing divisions obtain about 30 percent of their take-home income from incentives tied to return on investment (ROI) of their division. Second, outsourcing of parts is now possible with the overall expansion of the excavation equipment market. As the market became larger, more suppliers came to serve the market; and, increasingly, excavation equipment manufacturers pursued opportunities to outsource, even if this meant purchasing parts from their competitors. This trend is expected to continue.

You are a business analyst in the corporate office of CEML. The chief financial officer has asked you to investigate the transfer price policy and make recommendations, especially regarding the existing transfer pricing arrangement between the Winnipeg division and the Chicago division. The transfer of concern is a motor unit that the Winnipeg division assembles and uses in its own products; plus, it sells these motor units to the Chicago division. (See financial statements for the two manufacturing divisions, shown in Exhibits 1 and 2.)

The agreement between the two divisions has been in place for two decades, and from all indications there have been minimal problems. The Winnipeg division has always wanted the transfer pricing to be done on the basis of actual cost rather than standard. In contrast, the Chicago division has argued for standard costs for the transfer price. For the current year this transfer equals $75 million in revenue for the Winnipeg division and $75 million in variable manufacturing costs for the Chicago division. This transfer was done at standard variable costs plus 40 percent.

The Chicago division has been approached by a highly reputable manufacturer of engines with an offer of equal quality engine units at a price of $60 million. The general manager of the Chicago division wants to accept the $60 million external offer as it will increase the division's ROI. The Winnipeg general manager is opposed to losing the $75 million sales to the Chicago division. He claims that it would be difficult to replace the lost sales, which would be detrimental to the entire company. Moreover, he says, it would not be fair to set the transfer price at the lower $60 million as the Chicago division's higher ROI means that its general manager already has a substantially larger bonus. The Winnipeg general manager said he works about 100 hours per week, and a reduction in his bonus would be an insult.

The two general managers have not been able to reach an agreement. Starting next year the Chicago general manager plans to terminate the transfer agreement with the Winnipeg division and accept the external offer.

In undertaking your assignment, you investigate the offer provided to the Chicago division by the manufacturer of engine units. The vendor, Precision Engines Inc., specializes in engine units for the automotive and truck industries. Currently, those industries are in recessions, and Precision Engines has excess capacity. To supply the order to the Chicago division, you estimate that Precision Engines would have had to incur set-up costs to produce a new engine from their production facilities. After covering these set-up costs plus variable costs, you estimate that, with the quoted price, there would not be much left for fixed costs and profits.

The Chicago division has been considering the installation of a new production scheduling system. The chief financial officer also asked you to assess its viability. The new system will speed up shipments and, thereby, get the goods to the customers more quickly. The new equipment will cost $600,000, and it will have a life of 10 years with a salvage value of $100,000. The vendor will finance 80 percent of the value at six percent per year. As more goods will be shipped sooner, the division expects sales to increase by $200,000 per year. The main advantage will be that the new equipment will save $100,000 annually in labour costs. The cost of capital is eight percent, and the tax shield equals

$$\text{Tax Shield Rate} = \frac{T \times C}{C + R} \times \frac{2 + R}{2(1 + R)}$$

where
T = the income tax rate, 30 percent
C = the CCA rate, 30 percent
R = the cost of capital or required rate of return, eight percent.

Exhibit 1
Winnipeg Division
Operating Budget
For the Year Ending December 31
($ millions)

Revenue:	
Outside sales	$260
Internal sales	100
	360
Variable costs:	
Manufacturing	120
Administration	40
	160
Fixed expenses:	
Manufacturing	80
Administration	30
Research and development	40
	150
Operating income	$ 50
Working capital	$ 50
Net fixed assets	150
Investment	$200
ROI (50/200)	0.25

Exhibit 2
Chicago Division
Operating Budget
For the Year Ending December 31
($ millions)

Revenue:	
Outside sales	$400
Internal sales	50
	450
Variable costs:	
Manufacturing	170
Administration	30
	200
Fixed expenses:	
Manufacturing	100
Administration	40
Research and development	40
	180
Operating income	$ 70
Working capital	$ 50
Net fixed assets	175
Investment	$225
ROI (70/225)	0.31

Required

Use the case approach to address the tasks assigned to you by the chief financial officer.

Container Plastics

Ron Forlani has just gone public and expanded his container business. As a creative and skilled engineer, Ron develops technologically advanced machinery and moulds, which provide Container Plastics with a competitive advantage. Above-average profits come from the technological advantages, but only temporarily, as competitor imitation takes between six months and one year.

Ron has two tactics for addressing this technology copying. First, he plans and works towards continuously introducing technological improvements in processes and products. For example, there is an ongoing goal for production costs to decrease eight percent a year. Second, Container Plastics stresses new products. For example, there is a policy that 25 percent of the sales each year must come from products introduced in the past five years.

Container Plastics is in the plastic products industry, specifically in the rigid packaging sector. Its products include pop bottles, cosmetic jars, beverage cases, dairy cups and tubs, food trays, pails, and oil containers. In the industry, there are constant modifications and improvements in machinery and processes. Technology is becoming an increasingly important competitive factor in productivity, as are product quality and performance. The industry is being pressed to increase the use of higher-performance polymer materials, instrumentation, controls and automated materials-handling techniques in its processing operations. While these technologies continue to be generally available, they are more demanding in their implementation, operation and maintenance, reflecting a greater need for higher levels of labour and management skills. Such skills are generally scarce. This is not so with Container Plastics.

Container Plastics is one of the few Canadian organizations that has developed extensive research and development capabilities. The Canadian market is not large. However, the free-trade agreement with the United States, and the reduction in the tariff barrier that protected Canadian rigid packaging organizations, has forced Container Plastics to compete in a larger market.

In this larger market, competition is aggressive and persistent. In addition, waste disposal difficulties with plastics have placed pressure on the industry for solutions. Container Plastics and its competitors have reduced the amount of plastic used in given applications and developed means for economically recycling plastic materials.

Additionally, the trade association, the Society of the Plastic Industry of Canada, has a very active program to educate the public about the role of plastics in the environment and to implement viable technologies in Canada that will reduce the amount of plastic materials that eventually reside in landfill sites.

The performance advantages of plastics over competitive products assure their status as a material of choice in a wide range of applications. Due to the evolving global marketing strategies, including rationalization, and tougher competition from lower tariffs, the industry will not maintain the past rate of growth. Nevertheless, the growth rate will continue to exceed that for the Canadian manufacturing sector.

A technological advantage of Container Plastics is that production set-up can be done relatively quickly and inexpensively. Consequently, five basic moulding machines produce nearly 100 different products. This is a sharp improvement over earlier technology, which would have required 20 or more moulding machines.

Ron wants accurate product costing for profitable expansion. As the organization is new, he believes the time is appropriate for developing a costing system that is accurate and efficient. Ron has some understanding of job-order and process costing systems and standard costing, but he does not know what to use as the organization grows.

You have just been hired as the controller for Container Plastics and have learned the following about the company:

- There is a sales staff of eight persons, who are located throughout Ontario, Quebec, and the Northeastern United States. Agents are employed in Atlantic Canada.

- Sales persons contact clients, former clients, and prospective clients for orders. With product design engineers and the production scheduling manager, the sales person prepares a quotation.

- Generally, an order is for a certain quantity of a specified product. It will be for a future period, generally a year, with delivery being on a regular schedule or as requested if the client organization uses a JIT inventory system.

- Product pricing is a markup of 1,200 percent over cost, which is calculated as direct materials. All other costs are indirect. The markup gets reduced if necessary to obtain an order. Ron must approve all "markdowns", which he does automatically if the sales person requests.

- As long production runs reduce set-up costs, products are often inventoried for clients. There is no charge for this service.

As demonstrated in the operating statement (shown in Exhibit 1), the indirect manufacturing costs are many times larger than the materials costs. With 27 months of data, you run simple regressions to understand what drives the various indirect cost categories. The results of the regression equations are presented in Exhibit 2.

To maintain leading-edge technology, new equipment is constantly being considered. All proposed equipment for more than $10,000 is subject to capital budgeting evaluation. An example follows. Ron is concerned about whether the current approach is consistent with accepted NPV practices.

Exhibit 1

CONTAINER PLASTICS COMPANY
Operating Statement
For the Year Ended December 31

REVENUE		$43,152,750
EXPENSES		
Materials	4,226,740	
Machine room	15,071,788	
Warehouse	5,877,224	
Set-up	1,548,119	
Shipping	1,122,487	
Engineering	1,740,821	
Administration	1,950,298	
Selling and marketing	3,477,844	35,015,321
OPERATING INCOME		$ 8,137,429

Exhibit 2

	Dependent Variable	Independent Variable	Constant	Slope
1.	Set-up costs	Number of set-ups	$97,869	$2,721
2.	Set-up costs	Number of orders	$154,872	$482
3.	Warehouse costs	Square feet	$769,072	$7
4.	Warehouse costs	Size of order	$319,543	$0.54
5.	Shipping costs	Size of order	$54,912	$1.23
6.	Shipping costs	Number of shipments	$24,108	$374
7.	Machine room costs	Through-put time	$671,564	$119
8.	Machine room costs	Machine time	$974,653	$197

Note: For the constant or intercept, the t-value was equal to or greater than 2 for above equations 2, 4, and 5, and less than 2 for the others. For the slope or beta, the t-value was equal to or greater than 2 for equations 1, 3, 6, and 7, and less than 2 for the others.

Cost of equipment	($20,000,000)
Reduction in costs	
($2,500,000 per year after income taxes for the 5-year life of the equipment: $2,500,000 × 3.791)	9,478,000
Increased sales	
($2,000,000 per year less 30 percent variable costs and income taxes at 40 percent for the 5-year life of the equipment: $2,000,000 × 0.7 × 0.6 × 3.791)	3,184,000
Debt financing	6,000,000
Working capital	(1,000,000)
Tax shield from equipment	
($20,000,000 × 0.29)	5,800,000
Salvage value	
($4,000,000 at the end of year 5: $4,000,000 × 0.3222)	1,289,000
NPV	$ 4,751,000

$$\text{Tax Shield Rate} = \frac{T \times C}{C + R} \times \frac{2 + R}{2(1 + R)}$$

where
T = the income tax rate
C = the CCA rate
R = the cost of capital or required rate of return

Required

As the new controller hired to make Container Plastics a world class organization, use the case approach to put forth recommendations for a cost system that will help in accurately pricing quotations. Also, you are to make recommendations, if necessary, for improving the capital budgeting process.

Corral Recycling

Corral Recycling is a new company that provides commercial paper recycling solutions to small- and medium-sized companies in virtually every sector of Ontario. Clients include many professional organizations, car leasing companies, retailers, insurance companies, government and quasi-government organizations. Not all paper products can be simply dropped into a blue bin for recycling. Many paper products must be first shredded as they may contain confidential business, employee, or customer information.

Starting this mobile paper shredding service was straightforward. The main requirement was a five ton truck, an industrial paper shredder and a generator as a mobile power source. This type of mobile setup enabled Corral to shred paper right at the client's site and then take the shredded paper daily to recycling depots. The business required careful preparation or planning, as the investment to get the business rolling was substantial, and employees needed to be carefully trained and scheduled.

In just two years, Corral has gone from one outlet and two trucks to 14 branches and 39 trucks. All operations are in Ontario. A branch is nothing more than parking space for one or more trucks. This enables quick responses to clients who are not close to the Corral's office in Richmond Hill.

The organization consists of the president, who is also the chief executive officer. Her father is the chairman of the board of directors. In addition to her and her father, the board of directors consists of a lawyer from a legal firm in Aurora and an accountant who is the controller at a major Toronto-based Canadian retailer.

There are four vice-presidents reporting to the president. They are, respectively, responsible for sales, customer service, vehicle maintenance, and accounting/administration.

- The vice-president of sales is responsible for the sales representatives who visit prospective clients, and inside sales representatives, who deal with the needs of existing clients via e-mail and telephone. These employees work from the Richmond Hill office.

- The vice-president of customer service is responsible for the customer service representatives. This is the largest unit in terms of employees, who are located across the province as well as at the Richmond Hill office. Customer service representatives are the drivers who use the trucks to gather paper and, as required by the agreement, shred confidential papers. This vice-president is also responsible for scheduling the customer service representatives.

- The vice-president of maintenance is responsible for the fleet of trucks and ensuring they are in proper operating condition. Responsibilities include truck scheduling and truck maintenance. The latter includes all of the Richmond Hill mechanics, who repair the trucks in the vicinity of Richmond Hill. This vice-president must also arrange for maintenance and repair contracts for trucks that cannot be easily serviced by the Richmond Hill mechanics.

- The vice-president of finance and administration is responsible for all accounting, treasury, and administrative activities. You have recently joined Corral as the vice-president of finance and administration. You are a chartered professional accountant, whereas the previous incumbent, the brother of the president, did not have formal accounting credentials.

Corral uses a QuickBooks program for processing the accounting information. The accounting records are accurate and require little in the way of adjustments to prepare the annual financial statements. However, they are of limited use for decision making as data are records of what has happened and not very relevant for making decisions for the future. Consequently, the president has not regularly reviewed the operating statements of units with the respective vice-president. The budgeting module of QuickBooks has not been used. The president is content with the accounting information, but she is not pleased with the dismal level of profits. She wants you to assist her with improving profitability.

You examine the activities of the other three vice-presidents and learn that trucks and customer service representatives vary in the extent to which they are busy or, in other words, utilized. For example, because the vice-president of customer services schedules drivers and the vice-president of maintenance schedules trucks, there are times when drivers are scheduled without trucks, and at other times trucks are scheduled without drivers.

Another problem occurs when the vice-president of customer service schedules without consulting inside sales representatives. Without this information from clients via the inside sales representatives, client requests and circumstances get ignored.

Required
With the case approach, address the profitability concerns of the president.

Dennison Manufacturing International

"Growth opportunities are always accompanied by challenges," exclaimed the CEO of Dennison. She then went on to explain why you, a consultant, were hired.

Dennison started business in the city of Waterloo in 1951 as a manufacturer of televisions and electrical products. Television manufacturing was discontinued in the 1970s. Dennison remained in the electrical products business, which over time required it to enter many new markets. New products had to be constantly developed to maintain growth. The life of many of those products was short, and thus many products were exited after a few years. In addition, competition and the need to be cost effective obliged Dennison to locate new plants in China and India, and to enter into outsourcing arrangements. Along the way, Dennison also acquired about 30 small manufacturing plants. The result has been that Dennison now has 36 plants worldwide.

Systems integration attempts were a constant challenge because of acquisitions, outsourcing arrangements, and new product implementations. If there had been a uniform enterprise resource planning (ERP) system, the CEO said, there would have been fewer problems for you to resolve.

Sung, one of the older, larger divisions, has been subject to a series of problems, which the division's general manager and his controller have not been able to resolve. The CEO introduced you to the general manager and the controller. They explained that the sales have been lagging behind expectations, with the recently completed year being typical of the last three. A bigger problem has been that for the first year in decades, actual profits have become negative. You are shown the operating statement in Exhibit 1.

After a quick review of the operating statements, you asked if there have been any changes to the manufacturing process. You were told that the only change has been the use of a new supplier for the major components. The new supplier, EL Manufacturing, was an acquisition by Dennison that occurred late in the previous year. The acquisition was premised largely on EL being able to replace most of Sung's existing suppliers. The components from EL have defects, whereas the previous suppliers provided defect free components. Consequently, more materials and labour were needed, and rework and spoilage were charged to overhead.

Exhibit 1

SUNG ELECTRONICS DIVISION
Operating Statement
For the Year Ending December 31
(millions of dollars)

	Budget	Actual
Sales	842.0	823.8
Variable cost		
Direct materials, components	270.2	281.0
Direct labour	34.8	47.8
Manufacturing overhead	78.0	110.6
Selling	38.4	38.2
	421.4	477.6
Contribution margin	420.6	346.2
Fixed expenses		
Manufacturing overhead	196.4	264.4
Selling	42.4	42.2
Administration	74.4	74.6
	313.2	381.2
Net operating income	107.4	(35.0)

SUNG ELECTRONICS DIVISION
Modified Balance Sheet
As at December 31
(millions of dollars)

	Actual
Working capital	57.3
Net fixed assets	153.2
Investment	210.5
ROI, %	(16.7)

You ask for information on the cost of quality and customer satisfaction, and you receive the information shown in Exhibits 2 and 3. You are also informed by the divisional general manager that EL wants a higher price for the components being supplied to Sung. The general manager at Sung is opposed to any increase in price paid to EL because the market price is less than what EL currently charges. (You confirm with an independent source that EL is presently charging Sung five percent over the market price for the components.)

Two days later, the CEO introduces you to the general manger of EL. The financial statements for EL are contained in Exhibit 4. You learn that all of EL's production goes to Sung at a markup over costs sufficient to yield a 20 percent ROI, which is Dennison's markup for setting transfer prices between divisions. This arrangement started at the beginning of the year that just ended. The general manager of EL wants the markup to be increased in order to earn a 25 percent ROI, which he says is consistent with what is earned by other, independent

Exhibit 2

SUNG ELECTRONICS DIVISION
Cost of Quality Report
For Years Ending December 31
(millions of dollars)

	T	T$_{-1}$	T$_{-2}$	T$_{-3}$
Prevention	1.1	1.2	1.1	1.2
Appraisal	2.1	2.3	2.2	2.0
Internal failure	3.2	2.4	2.3	2.1
External failure	8.8	1.8	1.7	1.6
Total quality costs	15.2	7.7	7.3	6.9

Exhibit 3

SUNG ELECTRONICS DIVISION
Customer Satisfaction Survey
For Years T$_{-3}$ to T
(percent satisfied or highly satisfied)

	T	T$_{-1}$	T$_{-2}$	T$_{-3}$
Product quality	60.5	84.5	84.6	85.8
Durability	57.3	90.4	93.7	93.0
Good value	47.2	76.1	77.5	78.4
Features	61.0	69.3	70.4	70.7

Exhibit 4

EL MANUFACTURING
Operating Statement
For the Year Ending December 31
(millions of dollars)

	Actual
Revenue	147.4
Cost of goods sold	104.9
Gross margin	42.5
Selling and administrative expenses	36.4
Net operating income	6.1

EL MANUFACTURING
Modified Balance Sheet
As at December 31
(millions of dollars)

	Actual
Working capital	4.1
Net fixed assets	26.6
Investment	30.7
ROI, %	20.0

[Handwritten annotations:] not competitive — Alternative use ① Industry Benchmark to monitor whether EL can improve their manufacturing process a) defect (quality) b) market price (efficiency) ② switch to other supplier — 25% — lower price

firms making the same components. (You confirm that those other firms were earning 25 percent ROIs.)

Required

With the case approach, respond to the CEO's assignment to resolve the outstanding issues.

Dental Office

Rachael Branckowitz and Rick Young are dentists who are merging their practices into a partnership. In order to accommodate the expanded patient base, the dentists are looking at software packages to (1) keep track of patient records, (2) track the use of dental materials, and (3) handle the increased volume of payroll and other systems as the practice grows. The dentists have hired you as a consultant to advise them on software decisions.

You have familiarized yourself with the existing practices and the plans for the partnership. The new office will be in the Greater Toronto Area. The dentists plan to provide therapeutic, endodontal, and periodontal care. There will be four licensed hygienists, who will be responsible for dental hygiene procedures and patient education. Medical and administrative staff include four dental assistants, an office administrator, and a part-time accountant.

The clinic's operating capacity is expected to be 12,000 patient records. The current list of patients from both Branckowitz's and Young's practices combined amounts to 7,000 names. The information system should be able to handle up to the expected number of patients.

New patients contact the clinic either in person or by telephone. The receptionist or possibly the office administrator responds to the patient's inquiry. During the initial contact, the receptionist inquires as to the nature of the dental problem in the patient's opinion, or records symptoms, and collects the patient's contact and insurance information. If the problem is within the clinic's scope of care, the receptionist offers to schedule an initial appointment, determines the dentist and/or hygienists, and assigns an assistant and a dental facility.

Existing patients typically schedule appointments by telephone. Appointments also may be scheduled at the dentist's request as part of a treatment plan sequence. An appointment record should specify the following information: when the appointment will take place, in which room, the name of patient who will be treated, by which dentist, and with whom assisting, what dental procedure is scheduled, who made this scheduling record, and when and with what symptoms the patient contacted the clinic.

At the beginning of the first appointment, the new patient is requested to complete a patient information form consisting of 24 questions that aids in understanding the patient's state of health; the form also alerts the dentists and hygienists to allergies or blood-transmitted diseases. There is a preference to have this health history information in electronic form. It is to be attached to the patient record after the initial visit. The office administrator, receptionist, or dental assistants will enter the patient information into the system. In addition, the dentists want the system to be user friendly in the event that patients enter and access their medical history directly.

Required

You are to use the information in the case to design an information system at the Branckowitz & Young dental office to keeping track of patient records. Please use the case approach.

Digital-Imaging Robots

You and your sister have a good business idea. No, upon reflection, it is not only a good business idea, it is a great idea. You have 15 years of experience with robotics with an automotive manufacturer. Your sister has a decade doing digital imaging research. Together the two of you have designed the next generation of industrial robots, complete with patents and firm outstanding orders for at least three years. The essence of your business model is the advanced control module that is placed in a standard robot. Money does not seem to be a problem, with all the offers from angels (rich investors who provide money and advice to start-up businesses), VCs (venture capitalists), and IPO (initial public offering) specialists.

For a start, you and your sister envisage manufacturing 10,000 robots a year in a 50,000 square foot plant in Lethbridge, Alberta. Three hundred production workers will be needed to work on two shifts. The number of maintenance employees is expected to be 50. The most important group — engineers, programmers, and systems analysts — will be a group of 35 employees involved with the research, design, development and production of the control modules for the robots. As there are a limited number of firms with advanced robotic manufacturing operations, five sales engineers will be sufficient as long as they have an equal number of support staff. Accounting and other administrative staff are expected to number 45. This set-up with improvements in productivity would allow for production to increase by 10 to 15 percent a year over a decade. Adding a third shift would increase capacity by a further 40 percent. Details are shown in Exhibit 1.

To get the business going, you have been looking for a building. There is one that appears to meet your current criteria. Your real estate agent (i.e., your mother-in-law) wants you to sign for the building before it is "off the market"; she says it is a unique opportunity. However, you are not sure about making the commitment right now, despite the agent's persistence.

The management team will be headed by you as president and chief executive officer. Your sister will be the chairperson and the vice-president of research. Two vice-presidents will need to be hired, one for production, and the other for sales. Since your wife, a chartered accountant, was just fired from her job as a tax auditor, she could be the vice-president, finance and administration, as well as the CFO. Your sister's husband, a graduate in human resources, could be the vice-president, human

Exhibit 1

Operating Budget, Year 1 ($000,000s)

	Year 1	Description
Sales	$165.00	10,000 robots times $16,500 each
Annual labour costs		
Production	$ 18.00	300 employees times $60,000
Production maintenance	3.50	50 employees times $70,000
Research and design	3.50	35 employees times $100,000
Sales — outside	0.50	5 employees times $100,000
Sales — inside	0.20	5 employees times $40,000
Accounting, administration	2.70	45 employees times $60,000
Other production costs	6.00	
	34.40	
Other annual costs		
Executives	2.00	fixed overhead
Production	10.50	variable overhead, fixed overhead
Production maintenance	5.00	variable and fixed costs
Research and design	5.00	fixed costs
Sales	1.00	variable and fixed costs
Accounting, administration	2.00	fixed costs
Building, property maintenance	0.50	50,000 square feet times $10 per square foot
Other costs	6.00	
	32.00	
Operating income	$ 98.60	
Capital assets		
Building	$ 15.50	
Production equipment	55.00	
Production maintenance equipment	10.00	
Research and design equipment	16.00	
Sales equipment	1.00	
Accounting, administration	2.00	
Leasehold improvements	6.00	
Working capital	24.00	
	$129.50	

resources; his problem with authority figures would be unlikely to inhibit his performance.

As you and your sister work on the budget numbers for the new firm, you decide to visit the university from which you graduated in the hope of talking to one of your professors. Fortunately, he is in his office, and he remembers you; and he asks if you are still bullish on Dome Petroleum. (You had forgotten that recommendation. You sure believed in Jack Gallager. Too bad Dome Petroleum stock became worthless.) The office seems smaller than you remember, there are more books, but the professor, except for less hair, has changed little in 15 years. Teaching must provide a good life. You quickly explain your business plans and show him the numbers, as in Exhibit 1. Over the next hour, he asks you many questions. For some of the questions, you have answers, but for others, you do not. At 6:45 p.m., he says, "I must teach in 15 minutes. Can you and your sister meet me in my office tomorrow evening."

At the meeting on the next day, he says the following:

> Your strategy is to produce leading-edge industrial robots. Your competitive advantage is with the design stage. You are able to incorporate the latest research into the functioning of robots. However, this is but one activity in the value creation chain that leads to industrial customers that believe your robots provide advantages over all competitor robots. You must design all other activities in the chain so that they too achieve world-class performance. Consider outsourcing or application service providers for those activities for which you do not have a competitive advantage. You and your sister must decide if either or both of you will be active in management, or remain as designers and owners. Also, hire employees based on merit, not family connections.
>
> Consider your situation as a case question, and prepare for me a case response. Then I can be more explicit in addressing your proposed business undertaking.

He also provides you with information about a firm that makes extensive use of outsourcing for almost everything from sales to manufacturing, including research and development. That firm invested significantly in supplier assets, which it then linked to its customer assets using the Internet and its organizational know-how and systems. Consequently, the firm enables customers to access sales and service on its website. Its network of linked suppliers makes it possible for the company to efficiently tailor products to fit the needs of individual buyers.

He explains that with the Web for sales and customer service operations, the firm does not need a traditional distribution network standing between itself and its customers. Customers are served by a telephone or an online order taker who actually works for a supplier. Once placed by telephone or Internet, the order is sent to a co-ordinator — actually an employee of another company — who in turn passes the order to the plant. At the same time, the co-ordinator directs the suppliers to ship the parts to the plant. The co-ordinator also directs the parcel courier to the plant at the predetermined time to pick up and then deliver the finished product to the customer.

Moreover, this firm depends on its ability to optimize all assets that make up its business model, including relationships with employees, suppliers, investors, and customers. This clarity of business model is reflected in this other firm's above-average financial performance.

Required
Prepare a case response, as requested by the professor.

CASE 15

Dindal Air Conditioners

Dindal is a manufacturer of air conditioners for the North American market. It sells the Dindal brand through independent agents and produces units with the brand names of various retailers. Although largely an assembler of purchased parts at this time, Dindal does produce its own condensers. It also sells condensers to other manufacturers of air conditioners. Consequently, it has two operating divisions: condenser manufacturing and air conditioner assembly.

At one time Dindal produced nearly all of its own components. However, over the last 20 years, it has gradually switched from making components to buying them. Now it makes only a single component, the condenser. The switching to purchased parts was done gradually. Dindal wanted to make only those parts for which it had distinct competitive and strategic advantages.

The Dindal condensers and air conditioners are durable, efficient, and competitively priced. These product characteristics have been crucial for success, and they require efficient labour, competitively priced and high-quality parts, mistake-free assembly, minimal inventories, and on-time deliveries. Also, to remain successful the condenser division has an active research and product development team that is responsible for improving the products and manufacturing processes.

Once a year, the board of directors reviews divisional performance and assesses the company's future opportunities and threats. This is an informal occasion, but the directors — especially those with significant share holdings — are very serious about understanding the operations and achieving improved results. At this year's meeting, the directors were again unhappy with the performance of the assembly division. That division's general manager explained the poor performance as a consequence of the transfer price. The directors asked for a justification of the transfer price method and for regularly produced non-financial information on the performance of both divisions. You, as the president to whom the general managers report, have taken it upon yourself to resolve the board's concerns.

You first recognize that profitability of Dindal and its divisions has been positive and, over the last few years, largely comparable to the attached financial statements (shown in Exhibit 1) for the recent year. Each division reports as an investment centre, and the condenser division is clearly superior. Perhaps because of this unevenness of profitability, there is a dispute between the general managers of the two divisions.

Exhibit 1

DINDAL AIR CONDITIONERS
CONDENSER DIVISION
Operating Statement
For the Year Ending December 31
(in thousands of dollars)

REVENUE
Outside sales		$27,500
Assembly division		22,500
		50,000

VARIABLE EXPENSES
Manufacturing	21,000	
Administration	3,000	
Selling	3,000	27,000

FIXED EXPENSES
Manufacturing	7,000	
Selling, administration	3,000	
Research and development	2,500	12,500

OPERATING INCOME $10,500

Division Balance Sheet

Working capital	$ 4,000
Net fixed assets	26,000
Investment	$30,000

DINDAL AIR CONDITIONERS
ASSEMBLY DIVISION
Operating Statement
For the Year Ending December 31
(in thousands of dollars)

REVENUE
Dindal brand	$30,000
Other brands	22,000
	52,000

COST OF GOODS SOLD	31,000
GROSS MARGIN	21,000
ADMINISTRATIVE EXPENSES	7,000
SELLING EXPENSES	10,000
OPERATING INCOME	$ 4,000

Division Balance Sheet

Working capital	$ 6,000
Net fixed assets	36,000
Investment	$42,000

The condenser general manager wants a market-based transfer price. The assembly general manager wants it to be actual cost of goods sold plus 50 percent.

In reviewing the transfer price, you note that it is set at the average market price for long-term contracts to other assemblers of air conditioners. For the latest year, Dindal sold 110,000 condensers to outside customers, while the assembly division purchased 90,000 condensers. The assembly division sold 50,000 Dindal air conditioners, and 40,000 under other brand names. The bonus set by the directors last year was equal to 30 percent of a general manager's salary if their division's ROI exceeded 18 percent. The ROI is operating income divided by divisional investment. It was 35 percent for the condenser division for the latest year, but only 9.5 percent for the assembly division.

Required

As the president, use the case approach and prepare a report to the board of directors that addresses and resolves their concerns.

Do-It-Yourself Building Centres

Do-It-Yourself Building Centres (DIY) is a major regional home centre retailer with 27 stores, all located within two Canadian provinces. It competes with the market leader, Home Depot. Although Home Depot has a larger product range and lower average prices, DIY has carved out a very lucrative niche by serving homeowners who undertake renovation or construction projects.

Each DIY building centre has about 25,000 different products. A major part of its business is to provide advice to customers undertaking their own renovations and construction projects. The in-store sales associates devote a significant part of their time to providing free advice to customers. Among other forms of advice, this involved recommending the type of paint to use on the outside of a house compared to what to use on the interior, the type of stone and patterns for an interlocking stone driveway for a suburban home, etc.

The enthusiasm of DIY to provide assistance to customers has been so prevalent that the receptionists of individual stores have been obliged to provide advice or to pass the telephone calls on to the relevant associate on the sales floors. Although providing advice had been believed to be very successful in developing a loyal customer base and contributing to profitability, the calls were frequently disruptive. Associates were often busy with in-store customers at the time of the calls. Often, the calls were put through to inappropriate associates: e.g., a paint question was given to the fence and deck associate. In addition, calls that were put on hold were frequently lost as the reception telephone systems were not designed for call centre purposes.

To more effectively respond to customer requests for information, DIY established a dedicated call centre staffed from 8 a.m. to 8 p.m., seven days a week. The call centre is located in a small town in the southern part of the region. There is a 1-800 telephone number for callers holding a valid DIY credit card to access a variety of information services. The call centre associates are equipped with a telephone and Internet access to search for information on DIY products. These associates also have access to information on the Web pages of many suppliers. All calls are recorded.

As well as getting information on store locations and opening hours, callers are able to gain free advice on products and projects. They are able to ask questions about the tools and materials for projects and to get assistance from experts with solving problems with projects they are undertaking without the need to travel to a store. All call centre associates have extensive DIY store experience, with special training in renovations and construction projects. Part of their training includes associates actually undertaking DIY projects themselves. This means they can quickly understand and effectively answer customer questions.

You are the controller for DIY. The CEO has called you into her office. She is pleased with the new call centre. The satisfaction surveys have indicated that customers are very satisfied with the call centre services. However, she wants to know if the call centre is contributing to profitability. Specifically, she is concerned about whether the callers are actually customers, if the call centre service actually contributes to sales, if the benefits exceed call centre costs, and whether call centre costs can be reduced without impairing the service. At the present time, she wants to know what information is needed to address the above concerns and how to obtain that information. The other part of the project, to be done later, will require the gathering of the information. However, for this part the requirement is merely to determine what information is to be gathered and how.

Required

Use the case approach to respond to the CEO.

Electronic Process Equipment

Tom Simon developed a process control system in the early 1980s for an independent pulp and paper mill on Vancouver Island. He had been hired as the shift engineer, but realized that many of the operational problems at the mill could be solved with improved process controls. Although he had not set out to develop a process control system, he developed numerous individual process controls before he understood that the integration of all process controls into a system would improve the mill's operational efficiency and effectiveness. After designing and implementing the world's first integrated process control system for a pulp and paper mill, he was promoted to chief engineer. However, that did not satisfy Simon's urge to be creative.

In 1987, Simon, with two other young engineers, formed Electronic Process Equipment (EPE) to design, assemble, and implement process control systems for pulp and paper mills. Their first clients were British Columbia pulp and paper mills; then, after incorporating computers for better co-ordination, process control systems were sold to pulp and paper mills in Eastern Canada, to the states of Washington, Oregon, and Georgia, and to Norway. Subsequently, EPE expanded to all parts of the world where pulp and paper mills existed. By 1994, EPE was the world's leading process controls consulting engineering firm in the pulp and paper industry. The decision was made at that time to differentiate itself from all competitors by expanding into the research, development, and manufacture of leading-edge process control equipment. Then, in 1996, EPE expanded by providing process control systems to the petroleum and chemical industries.

Presently, EPE is employee-owned and highly specialized in designing and manufacturing or assembling process control equipment for customers located around the world in the pulp, paper, petroleum, and chemical industries. EPE provides a full process control service, from the initial design to the detailed engineering drawings, to the manufacture or assembly of equipment, and to its installation, testing, and ongoing maintenance.

EPE, as you would expect, has been dominated by engineers. All senior positions were occupied by engineers until 1999, when a chartered accountant was hired to be the vice-president finance. Since then there has been only one accountant among the engineers. Despite competition, EPE is now approaching annual sales of half a billion dollars, but there have been concerns with the cost accounting system. As a consulting management accountant, you have been requested to evaluate the existing costing system and recommend changes in order that the needs of EPE be met. Your approach to the assignment is to (1) understand the existing system, (2) understand the needs for a cost accounting system, (3) understand the shortcomings of the existing system with regard to the needs, and (4) recommend a cost accounting system that meets those needs.

To understand the existing system, you meet with the vice-president finance, who (1) describes the system in general terms, (2) arranges interviews for you with the controller, manager of cost accounting, and manager of budgeting, and (3) provides you with documentation of the existing system. With these sources you piece together descriptions of the existing cost accounting system, needs, and shortcomings.

Presently, there is a distributed accounting system that is provided by the same supplier that had been used with the earlier mainframe computer. This system is adequate for valuing inventory for financial reporting purposes and for preparing periodic financial reports. It has common data and account definitions across different business units so that financial managers can readily compare and consolidate financial results across multiple units and divisions. Complete financial statements are issued shortly after the close of an accounting period that require few, if any, post-closing adjustments. The statements are consistent with standards established by financial reporting, government, regulatory, and tax authorities; the system of data recording and processing has excellent integrity so that it satisfies stringent audit and internal control standards.

The existing system also reports individual product costs using variable and fixed cost classifications and responsibility centres used for external financial reporting, to value inventory and to measure cost-of-goods sold. The system provides financial feedback to managers and employees on the same reporting cycle used to prepare the aggregate organizational financial statements. The chart of accounts and database capacity allow a wide variety of special reports to be produced on the same basis as the financial reports.

You interview all senior managers plus middle managers in cost accounting, sales, and manufacturing. After 13 interviews, you conclude there is unanimous agreement that the existing system is adequately meeting the requirement for financial reporting. Nevertheless, there are two shortcomings with the existing system. First, the system is inadequate in estimating two areas: (i) the cost of activities and business processes; and (ii) the cost and profitability of products, services, and customers. Second, the system is inadequate in providing useful feedback to improve processes.

The first shortcoming arises from the assignment of costs to products and services. Direct labour hours are used to allocate indirect and support costs. Direct labour is not appropriate, because direct labour is not a high proportion of the company's manufacturing conversion costs. EPE has extensive automatic manufacturing processes. It also has shifted some of the costs of material acquisition activities (such as purchasing, receiving, inspection, handling, and storage) to a materials overhead pool; those costs are allocated to purchased items based on a percentage markup over purchase cost. To meet the needs of complex processes, multiple products and services, and diverse customers, EPE uses additional allocation bases, like material cost and machine hours. These modifications all assume that manufacturing indirect and support costs vary with the physical volume or number of the units manufactured. They fail to recognize that many expensive manufacturing resources are supplied to handle production of batches of items (activities required for set-up, ordering, receiving, moving, and inspecting products) and to design and sustain the myriad products the plant is capable of producing (activities required to design, improve, and maintain individual products). The cost system fails to capture the economies of production batches and product variety.

Another particularly devastating loss from the inaccurate cost system is that product designers and developers receive either no information or highly distorted information about the production costs of products they are designing. EPE's costing system forces product designers and developers to use obsolete and distorted information when making design choices and trade-offs. The erroneous choices and trade-offs made during this phase become locked in; they are costly and difficult to change when the actual cost behaviour is revealed during the subsequent manufacturing phase.

The cost system relies on responsibility cost centres for accumulating costs: both primary centres, where actual fabrication or assembly production work is performed, and secondary cost centres, such as indirect labour, maintenance, and tooling preparation, that provide services and support to the primary cost centres. However, assigning costs to responsibility centres gives little visibility to the costs of performing activities and business processes. Most activities and business processes use resources from many different cost centres. For example, it was noticed that an activity, like *respond to customer requests,* actually involved people from seven different departments. The customer service department, where the company thought this activity was focused, incurred only about 30 percent of the total cost of performing the total activity. The lack of information about the cost of activities and business processes has impeded EPE in setting priorities for eliminating inefficiencies, and makes it essentially impossible to benchmark activity and business process costs across units, either internal or external to the organization. Consequently, EPE often does not know where to focus total quality and re-engineering initiatives.

The present cost accounting system allocates manufacturing costs to products. However, the extensive costs for marketing, selling, administration, distribution, research and development, and general administration are not assigned at all to cost objects, such as products, services, and customers. This is because periodic financial reporting does not require or, in fact, allow these outlays to be assigned to cost objects. For financial reporting purposes, these cash expenditures are treated as period expenses. No attempt is made to causally link them to the activities and business processes actually being performed or to the cost objects — products, services and customers — that create the demand for or benefits from these expenditures.

As there are no financial accounting requirements at all for allocating indirect and support expenses to services produced or customers served, the service part of EPE's business does not merely suffer from distorted cost numbers; it has no cost numbers at all. There are responsibility centres for services, but there is no understanding of the costs of individual services and the costs by customer.

The second shortcoming is that the existing system does not provide adequate information to support organizational continuous learning and improvement. The present competitive environment requires managers and operators to have timely and accurate information to help them make processes more efficient and more customer-focused. The existing system prepares and issues summary financial feedback according to a monthly financial reporting cycle. Due to the complexities and adjustments associated with closing the books, the reports are delayed; though delayed only for several days after the close of the accounting period, it is still too late for responsibility centres to take immediate corrective actions. A production manager remarked:

> To understand the problem of delay and aggregated financial information, you could think of the responsibility centre manager as a bowler, throwing a ball at pins every minute. But we don't let the bowler see how many pins he has knocked down with each throw. At the end of the month we close the books, calculate the total number of pins knocked down during the month, compare this

total with a standard, and report the total and the variance back to the bowler. If the total number is below standard, we ask the bowler for an explanation and encourage him to do better next period. We are beginning to understand that we won't turn out many world-class bowlers with this type of reporting system.

In addition, the monthly performance reports for many operating departments contain extensive cost allocations, forcing managers to be held accountable for performance that is neither under their control nor traceable to them. The costs of corporate or manufacturing-level resources, such as the heat and lighting in the building or the landscaping outside, are allocated arbitrarily to individual departments despite the departments having no responsibility for these costs. For example, referring back to the bowling metaphor, think about the accountants, after a ball is thrown down each of the establishment's 35 lanes, counting every pin knocked down, dividing by 35, and reporting back the average (say, 8.25714) to every bowler. The number may be quite accurate (it does represent the mean number of pins knocked down per alley), but it is completely useless to an individual bowler. Each bowler wants to know the number of pins he or she has knocked down in order to improve on the next throw. A number has no value when it is influenced by actions of others who are uncontrollable.

Required

With the case approach, recommend a cost accounting system that meets the needs of EPE. Explain and justify your recommendation.

Foodco Restaurants

As a leading Canadian firm, Foodco has a restaurant division called Foodco Restaurants, which has seven branded restaurant chains. Foodco Restaurants has in the last five years completed acquisitions of various small restaurant chains. In the most recent year, acquisitions of restaurants accounted for 14 percent of the system growth. Existing restaurants only delivered two percent growth. The board of directors wants future growth to come from existing brands. In addition to top line or sales growth, the board of directors wants to reduce costs. They suggested a company wide cost reduction initiative.

Foodco Restaurants was established in 1883. It went through many changes to where it is now — one of Canada's largest restaurant operators. The seven operating chains or brands are as follows:

- Chicken Chalet, family/casual restaurant chain specializing in rotisserie chicken and barbecued ribs.
- Manny's, quick service restaurant chain serving hamburgers.
- Betty's Neighbourhood Bar & Grill, casual dining that provides guests with an innovative, varied menu featuring a fun environment.
- Dakota's Cookhouse, providing young families with fun, value and genuine hospitality featuring comfort foods in a wilderness lodge setting.
- Overland Steakhouse, casual dining featuring seasoned steaks, fresh fish, etc.
- Good Cup, leading specialty coffee retailer delivering superior quality, service excellence, and coffee passion.
- Millstone Grill & Bar, casual upscale dining that provides guests with familiar food and beverages.

Foodco Restaurants' strategies for growth are straightforward:

- Lever brands
- Drive geographic expansion
- Maximize supply chain leverage
- Increase organizational effectiveness
- Develop human resources.

A major component of these strategies is to examine existing chains to identify opportunities to improve cost effectiveness.

You have met with the general managers for the seven restaurant chains to introduce each of them to the cost-reduction project established by the board of directors. The basic information is available with Exhibits 1 to 7. In your discussions you wanted to understand the differences for sales and earnings, specifically between "company owned and managed" restaurants and those that are franchisee-managed and sometimes franchisee-owned. You learn that franchisees invest their own money, which allows Foodco Restaurants to finance more rapid growth.

You also learn from the general managers that the non–company-owned restaurants are less successful, as their levels of sales and earnings per store are usually less than the "company owned and managed" units. Franchisees, it was explained, are less willing to adopt the latest practices learned by the "company owned and managed" restaurants. When you ask for evidence of this sub-optimal performance, the general managers say that information is not systematically produced. Nevertheless, they all agree that restaurants not owned and managed by the company have inferior performance.

Foodco Restaurants has joined a group of owners of restaurant chains, which has hired a consulting firm to benchmark the performance of restaurants. The project was started during last year, and consequently only sales and earnings (before amortization of property, plant and equipment and interest expenses) benchmarks are available by restaurant type. (Note: Consulting firms often approach companies to establish industry performance standards. Each of these companies submits its financial information to the consulting firms, which develop benchmarks for the various types of industry. The information submitted by each company is kept confidential, but the consulting firms are able to present benchmarks as external performance standards. This generally would create a desire among the participants, individually or in group, to hire these consulting firms to benchmark their performance.)

Exhibit 1

Consolidated Statement of Earnings ($000,000s)

	Year T	Year T$_{-1}$
Systems sales*	2,400	2,105
Gross Revenue*	1,530	1,411
Earnings before the following	175	148
Amortization of property, plant and equipment	66	57
Interest expenses	9	7
Earnings before income taxes	100	84
Provision for income taxes	30	25
Net income	70	59

* Revenue recognition: Gross revenues include revenues from Foodco owned and operated foodservice activities. These activities consist primarily of food and beverage sales. System sales includes gross revenues as noted, together with the revenue from all franchised activities.

Exhibit 2

Consolidated Balance Sheet ($000,000s)

	Year T	Year T$_{-1}$
Assets		
Current Assets		
Cash	101	91
Accounts receivable	51	69
Inventories	28	29
Other current assets	18	15
	198	204
Property, Plant and Equipment	418	389
Goodwill	49	49
Brands and Other Intangible Assets	175	120
	840	762
Liabilities		
Current Liabilities		
Bankers' acceptances	32	52
Accounts payable, etc.	145	133
	177	185
Long-Term Debt	202	160
Other Long-Term Liabilities, etc.	83	66
	285	226
	462	411
Shareholders' Equity		
Capital Stock	33	31
Retained earnings	345	320
	378	351
	840	762

Exhibit 3

System Sales, Gross Revenue by Brand ($000,000s)

	Year T		Year T$_{-1}$	
	System Sales	Gross Revenue	System Sales	Gross Revenue
Chicken Chalet	740	393	704	393
Manny's	482	212	457	234
Betty's	371	268	322	243
Dakota's	222	191	151	118
Overland	75	75	62	62
Good Cup	312	155	238	176
Millstone	280	280	204	204
Interdivisional	(82)	(44)	(33)	(19)
Total	2,400	1,530	2,105	1,411

Exhibit 4

Earnings* by Brand ($ millions)

	Year T	Year T-1
Chicken Chalet	71	66
Manny's	43	35
Betty's	38	33
Dakota's	8	3
Overland	3	3
Good Cup	6	3
Millstone	11	8
Interdivisional	(5)	(3)
Total	175	148

* Earnings before amortization of property, plant and equipment and interest expenses.

Exhibit 5

Same Restaurant Sales Growth (percent)

Year	Chicken Chalet	Manny's	Betty's	Dakota's	Overland	Good Cup	Millstone's
T	1.2	1.8	(0.2)	0.7	(6.0)	(0.3)	3.1
T-1	2.7	3.0	0.8	(2.4)	(4.7)	4.0	0.8

Exhibit 6

Benchmark Results Per Restaurant

	Sales, $ millions		Earnings*, % of sales	
	Foodco Unit	Benchmark	Foodco Unit	Benchmark
Chicken Chalet	3.96	3.50	9.6	8.7
Manny's	1.37	1.10	8.9	8.4
Betty's	3.34	3.00	10.2	8.6
Dakota's	4.15	3.90	3.6	8.3
Overland	4.69	6.50	0.4	8.5
Good Cup	0.82	1.10	1.9	7.9
Millstone	12.2	15.00	3.9	8.9

* Earnings before amortization of property, plant and equipment and interest expenses.

Exhibit 7

Restaurants by Type of Ownership

	Company Owned and Managed	Owned and Franchisee Managed	Franchisee Owned and Managed	Total
Chicken Chalet	50	74	63	187
Manny's	58	125	168	351
Betty's	67		44	111
Dakota's	38		16	54
Overland	16			16
Good Cup	20	7	355	382
Millstone	23			23
Total	272	206	646	1,124

The consulting firm was able to analyze the performance of Foodco Restaurants chains to determine whether "company owned and managed" restaurants were superior to the franchised restaurants. The consulting firm reported that there was not much difference between the performance means (sales and earnings) of the two types of restaurants. However, it noted that the variance was very large for these chains. There were a relatively large number of poorly performing restaurants among "company owned and franchisee managed" and "franchisee owned and managed" restaurants. Equally, there were a large number of exceptionally well-managed restaurants, with above-average performance.

Required

You, the manager of management accounting, have been asked to scope out the project for reducing costs. Use the case approach to respond to the board of directors.

CASE 19

Fusion Computing

Fusion Computing Inc. is a two-year-old firm that has been growing rapidly through new product development and geographical expansion. The first budget was completed about nine months ago. Presently, the second budget cycle starts in a month. Now the CEO is reviewing the earlier experience in an attempt to make improvements to the budgeting process. You have been hired on a three-month contract to review the budgeting process, recommend changes to the board, and assist with the implementation of the next budget.

Substantial importance is placed on budgeting. Specifically, Fusion's strategic plans are implemented with the budgets. The goals and objectives of the strategic plans are budgeted or quantified and expressed as commitments. The acquisitions and use of resources are also explicitly budgeted. The budgets are, therefore, commitments to financial forecasts and agreements on expected outcomes.

Like any other planning activity, budgeting at Fusion helps managers focus on one direction chosen from many future alternatives. The CEO, with other members of senior management, defines the chosen path using some accounting measure of financial performance, such as net income, earnings per share, or sales levels in dollars or units. Budgeting is the tool, at Fusion, that managers are to use to successfully plan and manage operations and programs. Accounting based measures provide specific quantitative criteria against which future performance (also recorded in accounting terms) can be compared. Budgets are used as a standard for accessing actual performance.

Budgets were used to help identify potential problems in achieving specified goals and objectives. For the 12 month horizon, the managers in charge of responsibility centre budgets were expected to consider all possible events that might affect budgeted performance.

The results of the first budget are shown in the attached operating statement (see Exhibit 1) for the first nine months of this year. Currently, it is October 5. Fusion has a board of directors, a CEO and five vice-presidents. Two vice-presidents are responsible for product manufacturing. There is a vice-president for sales, another for research, and a fifth for finance and administration. The latter vice-president is responsible for financial accounting, budgeting, treasury, and other administration matters.

To carry out your assignment, you review the budgeting process from last year. It started on November 1. The management group (the five vice-presidents and the

Exhibit 1

FUSION COMPUTING, INC.
Operating Statement, Total Corporation,
For the nine months ending September 30 of this year
($ 000s)

	Actual	Budget	Variance
Sales	479,326	525,000	45,674 U
Cost of goods sold	321,669	300,000	21,669 U
Gross margin	157,657	225,000	67,343 U
Period cost:			
Sales	87,543	85,000	2,543 U
Administration	35,860	35,000	860 U
Research	67,159	40,000	27,159 U
Other	17,537	10,000	7,537 U
	208,099	170,000	38,099 U
Operating income	(50,442)	55,000	105,442 U

CEO) reviewed the budget submission during the first week of January. Some of the budgets had to be reworked before the management group met for the second time during the third week of January to approve the budget. The board met twice in February to approve the budget, which everyone agreed was highly satisfactory. Finally, the January to December budget was implemented last March 1, two months after the current year began.

You interviewed each of the five vice-presidents. Four of them supported the budgeting. Improvements were suggested.

One of the production vice-presidents said she was pleased to see the CEO actively involved, but noted he had a limited amount of time. As a result, the communication of basic process information was frequently overlooked, resulting in the need for revisions relatively late in the process. She prepared only one budget for her entire area, with the result that there was high unfavourable budget variance.

The other production vice-president said he had substantial difficulty in budgeting as the sales vice-president was very vague about the sales to be accomplished. In the end, he had to guess as to the sales and to create a production budget for that level of sales. He also said that as sales from his production plant were greater than the original budget, he should not be evaluated against the original budget. He prepared budgets for the eight responsibility centres for which he was responsible. These eight responsibility centres rolled up to the consolidated budget for all of his responsibilities.

The sales vice-president was concerned that the fixed 12 months for the budget would prevent her from preparing for emerging opportunities and threats beyond the original December year end. The firm was in dynamic businesses subject to significant changes.

The vice-president of finance and human resources advised you to talk directly to the controller and the treasurer, who were the two managers most involved with the administration of budgeting. The controller prepared the entire budget except for the cash budget. He said the process was evolving, and steps and procedures were becoming clearer to all involved. The controller had worked closely with the two production vice-presidents and the sales vice-president to ensure that the sales budgets were consistent with production budgets and that direct labour, direct materials, and overhead were consistently budgeted.

As Fusion was new to budgeting, there were many mistakes. The treasurer had difficulties with planning the receipt and payment schedules for accounts receivable and accounts payable. This was a result of the company having no experience on which to base future accounts receivable and accounts payable. The original cash budget proved useless, but continued to be used. Consequently, bank loans were accessed, and sometimes they were accessed when there was surplus cash.

The vice-president of research refused to participate in the budgeting; he claimed that budgeting would inhibit research creativity. The CEO prepared the budget for research.

Required

As the consultant, use the case approach to make recommendations for improving the budgeting process at Fusion Computing Inc.

Government Services

You are the newly appointed deputy minister of a provincial government department. There are 6,000 employees in the department, grouped into a corporate office plus six regions. Each region has a regional director. The corporate office has 400 employees, who provide policy development and centralized services.

Each region is an autonomous unit run by a powerful regional director. The power is in terms of certain political and community support. The minister and his cabinet colleagues want these regional empires reduced in power and brought under your control. There have been problems because the regions have been delivering programs according to the regional directors' wishes, rather than as legislated.

When you explain to the regional directors what you want done in the way of program standardization, they all agree, but nothing changes. You cannot terminate these regional directors, because they have many years of service, with performance evaluated as excellent for all recent years. The process of documenting poor performance, and by that terminating regional directors, would take years. These regional directors are all well paid, and unlikely to leave on their own. The story circulating is that they do not need to change, because you will soon leave, just like your predecessors.

You have a problem. You have promised the minister and the premier that you will standardize program delivery, but the regional directors who must do it for you will not co-operate. You have one year, or be terminated. As an "order-in-council" appointee, the minister can terminate you on short notice. However, you cannot terminate the regional directors in the same way, as they are appointees of the public service commission. You are at a loss for a solution. Responsibility accounting does not seem to work.

Required

With the case approach, put forth alternatives, evaluate their likelihood of success, select the most appropriate, and then suggest an implementation plan.

Harry Rosen

Last Tuesday morning you went with your boss to a breakfast meeting sponsored by the CPAs of Ontario. The purpose of the meeting was for CPAs (like your boss) to encourage prospective new members such as yourself to become CPAs. To encourage a turnout, there was a speaker, Mr. Larry Rosen, the CEO and president of Harry Rosen Inc.

Larry started with the following statement:

> We don't perceive ourselves as being in the clothing business. We don't just sell suits and sport jackets. It's a relationship-based business. My business is to get to know you, to have you build a relationship with one of my highly trained associates. I want to be your clothier for life. The whole key to our business is loyal clients. I strongly believe we have a corporate culture that has a love of quality and a love of clients. And building customer relationships is a managed process.

Larry's opening comments made you think of what you had read the previous night, when you had Googled "Harry Rosen".

> The company Harry Rosen was started 54 years ago by Harry Rosen, the father of Larry Rosen.
>
> — *Website for Harry Rosen Inc.*

> Harry Rosen Inc., a retailer of some of the most powerful brands in quality menswear, has built itself into a powerful national brand. That brand is based not simply on what it sells — because styles and designers change and fall in and out of fashion — but in how it sells. The brand provides a service promise to its customers, and this promise has been used effectively as a marketing and sales strategy to communicate the company's value proposition.
>
> — *The Deloitte perspective*

> The Harry Rosen chain is using [customer relationship management] technology the way it's supposed to be used, by creating an electronic concierge. What the company has been able to do is take what Larry Rosen's father used to do

personally for a much smaller client base and use technology to do the same thing for a much larger one.

— Ken Wong, Associate Professor of
Business and Marketing Strategy
Queen's School of Business

You have known Harry Rosen Inc. as an upscale men's clothing retailer with a relentless focus on the customer experience. You did not think you were old enough, as you had always considered Harry Rosen Inc. to be an "old man's" clothier. However, with Larry's statistics that the average customer was male and 39 years old, you now think you may have been wrong, and perhaps you are ready to be a Harry Rosen Inc. customer.

Larry spent about 45 minutes describing his company. It had been established by his father Harry and his uncle Lou in the Kensington Market area of Toronto with just $500 in start-up capital. Although men's wear was, and remains, a highly competitive business, Harry managed to make his firm stand out by establishing it in the minds of customers as a place where they could get their fashion questions answered. Larry said men are reluctant shoppers, and thus helping men purchase clothing was the way in which the company created a relationship. The focus of the relationship between associates (sales employees) of Harry Rosen Inc. and customers was on creating a confident image for aspiring customers. The relationship was developed through advice, trust, and continuity.

Harry Rosen Inc. has luxury stores. Presently, there are 16 stores across Canada and 700 employees. Traditional financial performance measures, such as sales growth and profitability, are important. Information technology is also important at Harry Rosen Inc. for two reasons. First, executives and buyers at Harry Rosen use data-analysis tools from Cognos Inc. built into a GERS Inc. merchandising system. The system offers more than a dozen sales and inventory reports for analyzing sales and helps the company identify sales trends, manage inventory, and calculate gross profit margins. Second, Harry Rosen Inc. uses information technology to maintain detailed customer information to better serve customers.

Harry Rosen Inc. has managed to become a household name in Canada, partly through the use of creative advertising to promote awareness and to cultivate a luxury image. One recent example is the company's teaming up with the Princess Margaret Hospital to promote a charity run for prostate cancer treatment. This has created substantial positive exposure in the Toronto market. There are plans to expand this charity run to other Canadian cities.

Larry Rosen also mentioned that the company hires for attitude and trains for skills. The advertisement depicted in Exhibit 1 attests to the importance of attitude and skills.

After Larry Rosen's presentation, you and your boss talked to him about the use of management accounting. Larry Rosen said that the management accountants were considering implementing a balanced scorecard. Your boss said that you had developed a balanced scorecard. Larry Rosen asked you what you would suggest for Harry Rosen Inc. in the way of a balanced scorecard.

Required
Using the case approach, develop a balanced scorecard for Harry Rosen Inc.

Exhibit 1

Harry Rosen Advertisement

POSITION:
Shoe Specialist Associates (Full Time)

REPORTS TO:
Store Manager

LOCATIONS:
Sherway Gardens, Etobicoke, ON
and Yorkdale Shopping Centre, Toronto, ON

MAIN RESPONSIBILITIES:
* To achieve and exceed sales and productivity standards
* Clientele development with respect to relationship selling in the Shoe Department
* Assisting in the maintenance of the Harry Rosen store image, in the Shoe Department and Stockroom inventory management
* Providing superior standards of service to all customers
* Provide feedback regarding Shoe Assortment and Selection
* Support with the Marketing and Product Knowledge Training

QUALIFICATIONS:
* Strong commitment to achieving excellence in the area of customer service
* Strong interpersonal skills
* Strong communication skills
* Professional attitude and appearance
* Footwear experience in retail/high-end sales preferred

Home Renovations

You have just become a shareholder of Home Renovations. Of the outstanding shares you own 10 percent, while Jean Paul Flynn, the founder, owns the remaining 90 percent. Mr. Flynn started Home Renovations 20 years ago with only himself. Now there are 15 permanent salaried employees, plus 200 to 300 trades persons on contract for 20 or more hours a week.

You are also the chief financial officer, controller, and office manager. You manage the five office staff, while Mr. Flynn manages the 10 estimators/project managers.

There is a strong demand for renovations. However, new firms are capturing most of this growth. Mr. Flynn suspects internal problems as the cause of Home Renovations not capturing its share of this growth. However, he is unsure about the problems and their resolution. He has allowed you to buy into the organization in the expectation that you will identify and solve the problems.

You devoted your first month to understanding the organization. The following paragraphs summarize your initial findings.

Homeowners generate renovation business by requesting an estimate for some renovation work. Examples would be a new roof, an external extension, rooms in the basement, and a wooden deck. Mr. Flynn sends an estimator/project manager at the first mutually convenient time. This meeting leads to a written quotation for the renovation, which is usually in competition with other renovators. If the quotation is successful, Mr. Flynn assigns the first available estimator/project manager. That estimator/project manager will hire the trades persons, such as plumbers, carpenters, cement makers, insulators, tillers, drywallers, and electricians for the various components of the project. The estimator/project manager will order the materials, which he will deliver or arrange for the vendor to deliver to the job.

Estimators/project managers are generally skilled in two trades, plus experienced in estimating projects and managing them to completion. In this dual role, they estimate the likely cost of renovation projects and manage them. The dual role ensures high utilization of time. Managing projects is a means of basing estimates on a thorough understanding of actual projects.

Renovation projects average $15,000. The average project requires a lapsed time of five weeks from start to completion, and three trades persons. Quotations would include a 20 percent markup for overhead and the project manager's time. Thus, the $15,000 job would be $12,500 for trades and materials plus 20 percent or $2,500.

Almost all the jobs are completed on time, but half exceed the cost estimate. When the project manager tries to collect on cost overruns, the customer often is reluctant to pay the extra. Generally only 20 percent of the overruns are collected. The remainder is written off. Last year these overruns reduced the operating income by half. Moreover, the request for additional money creates ill will and reduces repeat business.

You investigated the last 160 jobs, and found that 75 of them had overruns. Of the 75, 70 were where the person who managed the project was not the original estimator. Also, you noticed that all overruns were because of trade costs. There were no material overruns.

As you preceded with the investigation, you asked all estimators/project managers why they had overruns. Their explanations were that the projects were incorrectly estimated. They said the projects could not be completed within the cost estimate. Similarly, you asked each estimator/project manager why others were not able to bring their estimated projects to completion within the cost estimate. Their answers were that the other estimator/project managers did not always expect much from the trades when someone else estimated the project.

You then reviewed the process used for contracting trades. The office staff maintains a list of trades available for work. The system is based on trade type and equality. For each trade there is list, and the listed names are organized according to order of registering. When, for example, a cement maker is needed, the first name is chosen. If that person is not available, the name is placed at the end of the list (after the third "unavailable," a name is dropped). If available, the trades person is used, and his/her name is placed at the end of the list.

When assigned, the estimator/project manager tells the trades person what must be done and the completion date for key aspects of the project. A trades person usually works on two or three projects at Home Renovations simultaneously. This is necessary to average 20 hours of work or more per week. Weekly hours will vary with the number of active tradespeople on the lists.

The monthly financial statements are based on GAAP. Revenues are estimated based on the percentage of completed contracts, less incurred materials, trades, and period expenses, which include salaries and wages. The latter include all 15 employees, plus Mr. Flynn and yourself. The accountant calculates the profitability of each project at the end of the year. This helps with reassessing the markup for fixed overhead and profits.

Required

Using the case approach, prepare a report to Mr. Flynn analyzing the problems at Home Renovations and the recommendations that will resolve them.

Inner Streets Youth Drama Association

Seven years ago, Jean Nadeau formed Inner Streets Youth Drama Association (ISYDA) to help runaway and homeless youth to leave the downtown streets of a large western Canadian city. These young people have run away from home and dropped out of school. From the ages of 12 to 22, they are occupied with alcohol, drugs, petty crime, and prostitution. They are split almost evenly between males and females, and about 60 percent have at least some Native background. Most have no regular place to stay at night.

Jean had a similar background but had managed to leave the streets and get an education: first a bachelor's, then a master's degree in education, and finally a PhD. Despite having natural teaching abilities and a very high grade point average, Jean never became a teacher or professor. Instead, he started and remained with ISYDA, which had little financial support.

ISYDA believes that the problems of street kids are the result of painful experiences and low self-esteem. It also believes that these problems are solvable through self-expression and by taking charge of one's life. Drama is a vehicle for self-expression, and so ISYDA started drama groups in downtown social agencies frequented by the street youth. The youth developed skits and plays depicting their lives and problems. Through discussion among themselves and with audiences, they gained greater understanding of themselves, their families and their friends. ISYDA also started preventative programs in several junior and senior high schools where there were youth at risk of street lives. In these school programs, participants were referred by teachers. Referrals also came from fellow students. Community groups around the province began to request ISYDA plays and workshops and other sessions on how to develop similar drama programs.

ISYDA participants develop the plays themselves, with Jean or other facilitators helping in the process. Their drama concerns included issues such as drugs and prostitution on the streets and AIDS. ISYDA also has a residential program because participants in the drama programs often have no place to stay. The association rented a large house for sub-lease to some youth. It is for short-term accommodation for youth on social assistance. They pay for rent and food. Jean lives in the house, but the youth make the rules.

By teaching the youth to understand themselves and their situation, drama acted as a means of getting them off the streets. This worked in two ways. First, while in the group, they were off the street, at least temporarily. Second, the therapy achieved through drama helped them to resolve many of their issues, and so they became able to pursue off-the-streets alternatives, such as attending school, returning home, or obtaining employment. Due to its success in getting a significant number of young people off the streets either temporarily or permanently, ISYDA also became successful at raising funds for operations and capital expenditures.

There are five sources of funds. The first source is foundations that have in their mandates the support of social service activities such as ISYDA. This source supplies start-up or special undertakings, such as drama tours or drama camps. There is a limit to the number of years a group receives funding from this source. During ISYDA's middle years, it was the most important source of funds.

The second source is ongoing operational funding. This comes from several agencies funded by the government, and this funding signifies an acceptance of the importance and effectiveness of an agency. About two years ago, ISYDA began receiving this funding for about half its operating costs; this is currently its largest source of funding.

The third source is federal and provincial employment grants, at minimum wage rates. This was the most important source of funds in the first few years of ISYDA; then the grants paid Jean and the facilitators. More lately, they pay youth to obtain work skills.

Fourth, performances and workshops generate money. ISYDA, the youth performers, and support staff share this money. Some years, depending on the particular plays and talents of the actors, this has been as much as 20 percent of total revenues.

The last source is donations. These funds can come from individuals or groups. For example, a local technical college repaired extensively a $1,000, 15-person van for the wholesale cost of parts. A service club donated the other van. (ISYDA records the market value of donations as revenue.)

ISYDA is a dynamic organization, carrying on a multitude of flexible programs that respond to the youth clients and their circumstances. Each program constitutes an organizational unit or responsibility centre. Each program has a set of definite expectations, e.g., method of operation, number of clients, and client progress by period. It is the organizational formulation of these expectations for helping street youth that entices support from funding agencies.

Jean sees the structure capturing the special attributes of ISYDA, as noted in the chart in Exhibit 1.

ISYDA has been successful both with helping street youth and with raising funds. Exhibit 2 shows the expenditures for the latest year. Jean is the only full-time employee. He hires part-time facilitators and administrators as needed. The focus is on helping the clients and not on a permanent organization. A lean organization is is crucial to avoid deficits.

Each program has detailed and accurate records as funding agencies require feedback on how their monies were spent and the results accomplished (i.e., the number of youth helped). The youth are readily identifiable by program, and so is the funding. However, expenditures can be direct or indirect. The direct costs are the hours an employee devotes to a program as a proportion of his or her work day times total remuneration. Other direct costs would include materials, any monies paid to the youth for performances or practices, and snacks. (Provision of snacks has always been a component of programs, as many youth are living in atypical settings. They often come to practices and performances hungry. The snack may include a restaurant meal when on tour — i.e., McDonalds — but most often includes the purchase of food to prepare sandwiches or even a hot meal.)

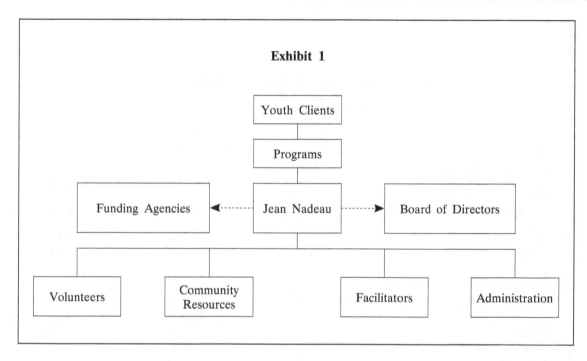

Exhibit 1

Indirect costs are more difficult to allocate, and some are even joint. Gasoline and other transportation costs are usually difficult to allocate, but the travel record could be used to allocate them to programs. Each travelled kilometre relates to a program.

You have recently joined the board of directors as the (volunteer) treasurer. In the meetings you have had with the board, funding agencies, and Jean, there have been suggestions that there are shortcomings with the accounting information. An executive director of one of the larger funding agencies put the problem succinctly when she said, "We provide ISYDA with money, but we are not sure where the money goes. Sure, for the programs we are funding, we get client numbers and their progress. We appreciate this. However, we would like to know how the money is spent within the programs we fund." ISYDA submits financial statements for the total organization to all funding agencies. Sometimes this pacifies them, but some request more specific information, which requires hurried projects for allocating costs to individual programs or sub-programs.

With this concern in mind, you review the accounting system with Jean and a volunteer, who inputs the financial transaction data with a computer accounting package. The accounting format is for a single entity. Nevertheless, the package being used has the capacity to report revenues and expenses for 10 programs plus consolidating. Exhibit 2 shows the financial statements for ISYDA.

You note that there are nine different programs, as shown below:

- Riverbend Community Centre
- J.J. Laurier Drop-in Shelter
- Southwest High School
- Southwest Junior High School
- Crump Junior and Senior High School
- Northern Tour
- Central Tour
- Summer Camp
- House

Exhibit 2

INNER STREETS YOUTH DRAMA ASSOCIATION
Income Statement
For Years Ended December 31

	T	T$_{-1}$	T$_{-2}$
REVENUES			
Government funding	$ 60,000	$ —	$ —
Foundation grants	22,000	42,000	21,000
Performance, workshop	10,905	9,652	9,876
Employment grants	7,305	17,854	10,554
Rent	5,400	1,700	—
Donations	6,940	21,893	2,575
Total	112,550	93,099	44,005
EXPENSES			
Salaries, benefits	33,100	30,600	20,000
Contract employee payments	27,500	25,500	9,500
Transportation	24,250	21,200	9,000
Snacks	3,200	2,500	3,500
Rent on house	11,100	4,900	—
House utilities, repairs	3,500	1,900	—
Food at house	4,200	1,500	—
Administration	5,100	4,400	2,300
Total	111,950	92,500	44,300
NET REVENUE	$ 600	$ 599	$ (295)

INNER STREETS YOUTH DRAMA ASSOCIATION
Balance Sheet
As of December 31

	Year T	Year T$_{-1}$	Year T$_{-2}$
ASSETS			
Cash	$10,050	$ 5,000	$ 1,000
Accounts receivable	9,450	10,000	8,000
Inventory, supplies	150	100	50
Prepaid rent	900	900	—
Fixed assets, vehicles, net	20,500	15,500	1,000
Total	$41,050	$31,500	$10,050
LIABILITIES			
Accounts payable	$ 1,500	$ 2,000	$ 1,000
Unearned revenue	38,146	28,696	8,845
SURPLUS (DEFICIT)			
Accrued to current year	804	205	500
Current Year	600	599	(295)
Total	$41,050	$31,500	$10,050

Required

The board of directors asked you to address the concerns of the funding agencies for regularly produced accounting information by program. Be specific regarding individual expenditures and accounting practices, and use the case approach.

King Coal

The provincial government's electrical utility has a coal mine in the King region that produces thermal and metallurgical coal using an integrated pit mine and cleaning plant. Separate reporting is not done for the extraction and cleaning plant or for the thermal coal and metallurgical coal. The assumption is that if the total cost is competitive, then each part must be efficient. Although this may have been a reasonable approximation in the past, new mines have been opened that are more efficient. Now the utility's senior management wants to manage the cost of each part individually.

The controller has assigned you to calculate the profitability of the operations. The reason for your assignment is to figure out, as accurately as possible, the exact costs of each coal (thermal and metallurgical) and each operation (extraction and cleaning) at the King Mine. Then you are to compare the costs with other operations of the utility and with industry averages. These costs will be the starting points for specifying annual improvements in productivity and cost effectiveness. A component of this study will be to devise a transfer price between the extraction and cleaning plant, if that would motivate cost effectiveness. When he assigned the project, the controller conveyed the transfer price idea of a board member, but admitted he does not understand why it would be beneficial. The controller asks that you explain transfer pricing and its possible benefits in your report.

The production process includes the extraction and hauling of raw coal to the cleaning plant. The cleaning plant prepares both types of coal for shipment by rail, the thermal to a thermal plant and the metallurgical to a private steel mill.

The financial performances of the extraction and cleaning operations and expenses of the ancillary support and administrative activities combine into a single operating statement. The statement is shown in Exhibit 1. You realize that to accomplish your project you will need to allocate these costs to the two types of coals and two operations. Subsequently, you arrange appointments with managers and other employees who are knowledgeable concerning the content and drivers for each expense line item.

Employees are transported by company bus from two towns where they live to the mine site. The last 27 kilometres into the mine is a company-maintained road.

You find that the annual contract for thermal coal is 450,000 tonnes, and 150,000 tonnes for metallurgical coal. For each contract, the King mine is the prime supplier, and the customers make up any shortage by alternative and more expensive secondary suppliers. The mine ships the full amount of each contract for each year.

Exhibit 1

KING MINE DIVISION
Operating Statement
For the Year Ending December 31
(in thousands of dollars)

REVENUE
Thermal coal		$ —
Metallurgical coal		11,700

EXPENSES
Extraction wages and benefits	$10,500	
Plant wages and benefits	9,500	
Diesel fuel, gasoline	3,800	
Amortization, pit trucks, equipment*	3,000	
Amortization, buses*	900	
Amortization, plant equipment*	2,800	
Amortization, depletion costs	800	
Management salaries and benefits	2,700	
Administration	2,300	
Facilities, utilities and taxes	2,600	
Marketing department	800	39,700
Net income before income taxes		$(28,000)

* Amortization is based on the physical exhaustion of the asset.

The metallurgical coal generates revenue at the rate of $78 per tonne. The thermal coal does not generate revenue, because it is shipped to a thermal plant owned by the provincial government. To estimate a transfer price, you asked the general manager of the thermal plant what would be the landed cost of thermal coal on a long-term contract. She estimated the cost to be $71 per tonne (delivered) for comparable coal. The traffic officer (responsible for arranging for and monitoring transportation) explained that King ships clean coal at the cost of $6 a tonne.

The mine is a series of interlinked pit mines that produce 652,000 tonnes per year. Excavation equipment and trucks remove the overburden. The pits differ by coal type, and for efficiency purposes the miners extract thermal coal for three weeks, and then metallurgical coal in the fourth. Pit mining wages and benefits, amortization for pit trucks and equipment, and depletion costs are entirely attributable to the extraction of the coal. These costs are the same per tonne for both thermal and metallurgical coal.

Shrinkage in the cleaning plant through the elimination of impurities reduces the weight by eight percent. The expenses for the cleaning plant include plant wages and benefits and amortization for plant and equipment. The metallurgical process has additional stages and, thus, a higher cost per tonne than thermal coal. You estimate that 70 percent of all cleaning costs are attributable to thermal coal, and 30 percent to metallurgical coal.

As for diesel fuel and gasoline expenses, you estimate that $3,500,000 was for extraction, $150,000 was for the loaders in the plant, and $150,000 was for the buses.

There are nine buses scheduled to drive back and forth between the two towns and the mine site where all employees report for work; 500,000 kilometres were driven last year. Employees take the bus about 98 percent of the time. The following table shows the breakdown of employees by department:

Extraction	41%
Plant	26
Management	13
Administration	15
Marketing	5

When analyzed according to where they work or how they devote their average work day, the management, administration, and marketing personnel had the following to say in aggregate:

	Extraction	Plant	Neither	Total
Management	45	35	20	100%
Administration	45	40	15	100%
Marketing	—	—	100	100%

About $600,000 of the administration expense item is attributable to buses. Square feet occupied is the cost driver for facilities, utilities, and municipal taxes. You calculate the allocation to be 45 percent for extraction, 35 percent for plant, 10 percent for administration, 5 percent for management, and 5 percent for marketing.

Required
Complete your assignment using the case approach.

CASE 25

Major Electronics

Major Electronics is a multi-plant assembler of computers and computer products. It has 40 plants located in southern Ontario and greater Montreal. In recent years, there have been concerns that its traditional method for allocating manufacturing overhead (MOH) is no longer relevant. Direct labour costs now average 6 percent of manufacturing costs for its 40 plants, with 55 percent for direct materials, and 39 percent for manufacturing overhead.

The corporate management accounting branch is investigating alternative cost drivers. MOH is divided into three groups: procurement, production, and support. The standard chart of accounts for Major further classifies these costs into sub-classes (see Exhibit 1), which are ranked in order of importance.

The corporate management accounting branch surveyed manufacturing managers at all 40 plants to obtain a list of the most important cost drivers for MOH.

Exhibit 1

Sub-classification of Manufacturing Overhead Costs

Procurement	Production	Support
• Stores	• Direct labour payroll taxes and benefits	• Production engineering
• Purchasing	• Occupancy	• Process engineering
• Materials	• Direct labour supervision	• Manufacturing management
• Engineering	• Other indirect labour	• Quality assurance
• Materials management	• Operating expenses	
• Production control	• Amortization	
• Material specification	• Production management	
• Inbound freight	• Equipment expenses	
• Traffic and receiving	• Shipping	
• Corporate materials charges		

Cost Driver	Total MOH	Procurement	Production	Support
Total manufacturing space	0.57	0.32	0.50	0.49
Average total head-count in manufacturing	0.86	0.44	0.81	0.56
Direct labour dollars	0.73	0.12	0.77	0.45
Direct material dollars	−0.17	−0.12	−0.44	−0.30
Number of part numbers	0.13	0.45	0.16	−0.06
Percent of parts inspected on receipt	0.00	0.24	−0.11	0.16
Number of products	0.53	0.19	0.50	0.59
Number of customer orders per month	−0.05	−0.04	−0.07	0.08
Average cycle time in days	0.10	−0.21	0.19	0.21

Exhibit 2

With these cost drivers, an analysis was done to ascertain their correlation coefficient (r) with MOH in total and each of the three major groups. Each r is shown in Exhibit 2.

These results were presented to a group of plant managers that was formed to provide advice to the corporate management accounting branch on the development of alternative cost drivers. The committee was not surprised at the correlations. However, they had two concerns that could not be immediately resolved. First, the committee was unclear about how a positive r in regression analysis implied that the respective costs were driven by a cost driver. With regression analysis, there is a constant (or alpha or intercept) and a slope (or beta). The slope coefficient is comparable to variable costs per unit of the cost driver. The constant is comparable to the fixed costs. Many members of the advisory group were puzzled about whether total indirect costs from a pool should be allocated, or just the variable costs. Second, some overhead costs have been incurred for capacities much greater than current production. For example, in most plants the materials specifications units operate at 50 percent of their full capacity. Many members thought underutilized capacity should not be allocated to existing products. It was thought that this would not be fair when facing competitors that were operating at full capacity.

Required

As the project manager for the alternative cost drivers project, prepare a report using the case approach that makes recommendations for a successful project.

CASE 26

Modern Chair

You have just started working for Modern Chair, a new organization that uses a modern, automated approach to the manufacture of a variety of chairs. Using computer-assisted design specifying and ordering materials and scheduling manual and machine activities, every chair can be unique, and Modern Chair can offer individual design on demand. Modern Chair controls costs, which are lower than those of competitors who have less automation and less ability to efficiently produce small batches. Nevertheless, the success of the company has led to a problem. Currently, with the economy in what looks to be a temporary boom, there is a shortage of capacity. There are no plans to expand production capacity to meet temporary excess demand. The president asked you for recommendations for making the best use of limited production capacity. Your recommendations are to facilitate profit maximization.

In your investigation, you realize that there is not much in the way of information on which to base the recommendations. The organization has little history, and the president has personally made all important decisions. You note, however, that besides the design department that has unlimited capacity, there are two production departments: the first department assembles the chairs, while the second does the finishing. Although there are 252 different types of chairs if all styles and finishes are considered, Modern Chair divides them into two types, upholstered and straight back.

Using this conceptualization, you allocate production costs according to assembly or finishing. Within each department, you further divide the costs according to upholstered or straight back chairs. You then take the cost for each product category in each department and run simple regressions, and you get the results seen in Exhibit 1.

Each department's total available hours are 3,920 hours a year, i.e., 16 hours a day for five days a week for 49 weeks a year. The assembly department runs five identical lines. The yearly capacity is 19,600 operating hours. The finishing department runs four lines for 15,680 hours of available time. An average upholstered chair sells for $147, and the average straight back chair sells for $76. Sales of straight back chairs are unlikely to exceed 25,000 at that price, while that price will restrict upholstered chairs to 25,000. There is sufficient capacity in the assembly department, but not in the finishing department.

Exhibit 1

Variable	Coefficient	Standard Error
ASSEMBLY DEPARTMENT		
With the total costs of upholstered chairs as the dependent variable		
1. Constant	$ 98,747	$246,868
Independent variable: Time in production hours	$27.14	$11.81
$r^2 = 0.55$		
2. Constant	$352,363	$167,922
Independent variable: Direct labour hours	$11.74	$10.67
$r^2 = 0.33$		
With the total costs of straight back chairs as the dependent variable		
1. Constant	$347,428	$386,031
Independent variable: Time in production hours	$21.11	$ 6.60
$r^2 = 0.61$		
2. Constant	$797,318	$346,660
Independent variable: Direct labour hours	$ 5.06	$ 5.62
$r^2 = 0.35$		
FINISHING DEPARTMENT		
With the total costs of upholstered chairs as the dependent variable		
1. Constant	$ 27,957	$ 8,223
Independent variable: Time in production hours	$ 4.74	$ 1.16
$r^2 = 0.67$		
2. Constant	$ 54,819	$ 10,542
Independent variable: Direct labour hours	$ 3.51	$11.70
$r^2 = 0.31$		
With the total costs of straight back chairs as the dependent variable		
1. Constant	$155,850	$141,682
Independent variable: Time in production hours	$ 6.18	$ 1.29
$r^2 = 0.50$		
2. Constant	$347,310	$ 86,828
Independent variable: Direct labour hours	$ 3.57	$ 2.75
$r^2 = 0.33$		

For each department, the standard hours in production needed to produce the chairs are as follows:

	Upholstered	Straight Back
Assembly	0.75	0.50
Finishing	0.45	0.75

Modern Chair occupied its current facilities four years ago. The assembly department cost $927,000 for plant and equipment. The finishing department's plant and equipment cost $554,000. About 80 percent was for equipment, while the remaining

20 percent was for the land and buildings. Since then, the capacities of the two departments have increased about five or six percent a year. The managers and employees found ways to increase efficiency and effectiveness.

In examining the non-manufacturing costs, you find that they are all fixed except the five percent sales commission paid on the sales price of each chair.

Required

You have just finished a nice lunch at Spartan's and are seeing the President of Modern Chair within an hour. Linear programming comes to your mind as being a suitable tool. What analysis and recommendation would you provide? Use the case approach.

Pasta, etc. Family Restaurants

You are a member of an independent consulting firm that specializes in serving the restaurant industry. Unlike many consulting firms that are extensions of audit firms, your firm has serious and in-depth expertise with the restaurant industry. The following is a typical assignment.

"Pasta, etc." is a chain of Italian casual dining restaurants located in southern Ontario. The restaurants are at the top end of the casual dining segment; guests are offered many of the benefits of fine dining without the formality. The menu is limited to approximately 20 entrees to ensure a high level of execution and service. Menu items such as steaks, pork chops, ribs, roast beef, chicken, seafood and salads are complemented by a wide assortment of alcoholic and other beverages.

The chain is only five years old, but already there are 74 outlets. The owners had planned to expand the number of outlets to 100 in Ontario over the next two years and then expand across Canada and into the United States. However, recent performance has been disappointing.

Some background is useful. The Torra family arrived in Toronto from Italy in 1955. Tony worked in an Italian restaurant immediately upon arrival in Canada. After one year he started his own restaurant, which provided him and Enza and their two children with a very good livelihood. Both boys — Joe and Donnie — went to university. Joe became a high school mathematics teacher, while Donnie became a dietician and joined the family restaurant.

As the original restaurant was not large enough for Tony and Enza, plus Donnie with his growing family, Donnie persuaded the other members of the family that expansion was necessary. It took three years to convert the original restaurant into an expansionary "model restaurant" that would be relatively simple and, therefore, could be managed by a non-family member.

The excitement of expanding the family business encouraged Joe to give up teaching high school mathematics in order to return to the family business. In the following five years, Joe and Donnie went from one to the current 74 restaurants. They are now wondering what happened.

Exhibit 1

Operating Statement ($ 000s)

as % of sales

Variance = Actual − Budget / Budget × 100%

	Budget	_as % of sales_	Actual	
Sales	$2,900		$3,060	6 %
Variable cost of sales				
Direct materials	500		713	43%
Direct labour	900		1,126	25%
Variable overhead	200		257	29%
	1,600	x	2,096	31%
Contribution margin	1,300	x	964	26%
Fixed costs				
Other labour	150		152	1%
Rent	200		197	2%
Utilities	150		157	5%
Miscellaneous	50		46	−8%
	550	x	552	0%
operating income = Net Income _before interest and taxes_	$ 750	x	$ 412	−45%

_−33%_

All 74 restaurants are basically the same. Sales have exceeded expectations, but profits are much less than expected. There is some variability in sales among the 74 restaurants. There is a scheduling model that, based on sales, assigns the optimal number of employees to be on staff for each restaurant (i.e., restaurants with higher sales will require more employees in order to maintain service quality). The planning, budgeting, and financial reporting systems are meeting current requirements. Employees are remunerated with basic wages, plus incentives tied to sales. These incentives account for about 20 percent of the average employee's remuneration, and thus there is a keenness among employees to maximize sales.

In your consulting assignment, your focus is with what is going wrong with the restaurants. You suspect operational problems; thus, you and your associates study a random sample of five of the 74 restaurants. All five are very similar, with the restaurant in Exhibit 1 being representative.

As Joe and Donnie cannot agree on the reasons for the profit shortcomings, and thereby on the solutions, your consulting firm has been hired. Joe believes that sales improvements will solve the profit shortcomings. Donnie, in contrast, believes the inadequate cost control has caused the profit shortcomings. However, neither has been able to gather convincing evidence.

Pasta, etc. is fortunate in having a specialized restaurant enterprise resource planning (ERP) system that has the potential for linking all systems. Although the potential of the ERP system is just starting to be utilized, it can calculate the price and variable costs for the 20 entrees that are being sold. This information is shown in Exhibit 2.

Exhibit 2

Price and Variable Cost Per Entree

	Price Per Entree	Variable Costs per Entree
# 1	$27.50	$20.25
# 2	24.75	18.05
# 3	24.00	15.24
# 4	19.75	13.04
# 5	19.50	8.39
# 6	17.50	7.90
# 7	12.00	6.59
# 8	11.25	7.88
# 9	19.75	9.94
#10	8.50	4.09
#11	13.00	9.44
#12	21.50	13.74
#13	17.25	9.86
#14	14.00	8.23
#15	20.50	13.75
#16	18.00	6.71
#17	14.50	7.62
#18	10.00	4.85
#19	14.50	7.42
#20	19.75	10.67

Required

Use the case approach to identify and solve the profit problems facing the model restaurant.

Persaud Products

You are the vice-president of manufacturing for the Persaud Products Company, which makes products for wireless communications. The majority owners started the company to manufacture products based on their inventions and patents. The company has grown rapidly over its three years of existence.

The company consists of five departments: human resources (HR), manufacturing, research, sales, and finance and administration. Manufacturing uses the latest equipment, systems, and technology to produce the products invented by the research department.

In the last few years the company has increasingly formalized its management systems. For example, the department heads of the HR, manufacturing, and research have co-operated to develop techniques to measure and forecast performance. The department heads for sales and finance and administration have developed a budgeting system. The new budgeting system, however, has made your department (manufacturing) look unfavourable.

Units within the HR, manufacturing, and research departments have set longer-term, aggregate goals based on benchmarked performance measures such as return on capital. The elements or factors measured are key performance indicators (KPIs) such as profit, cash flows, cost ratios, customer satisfaction, quality, and time to market. The performance criteria for benchmarking are the performance of internal or external peer groups and the results from prior periods. In addition, the company's units in HR, manufacturing, and research are measured and rewarded on the basis of how well they reduce fixed costs and improve uptime (e.g., the time that a piece of equipment is working — the opposite of downtime) in comparison to best-in-class industry benchmarks.

Empowerment has been expanded. Employees are free to make mistakes and equally free to fix them. Managers have significant discretion in making decisions. Consequently, managers can obtain resources more quickly than in traditional companies and without the need for elaborate documentation, partly because they are accountable for the profitability of their units and can, therefore, be expected to reduce any excess expenses in the event that demand falls. In such a system, the "spend it or lose it" practice that exists in traditional business has no meaning.

The KPIs tend to be financial at the top of the department and more operational the nearer the unit is to the front line. It has been found that KPIs do not need to be precise to be effective.

Rolling forecasts for the next 12 months play an important role. The forecasts, generated each month, help managers to continuously reassess current action plans as market and economic conditions change.

The budgeting system is even newer than the company. Participation is emphasized throughout the budgeting update process until the budget is approved by the president and CEO, Kim Persaud (who is also in charge of sales). Kim approves the additional monthly budget herself before submitting it to the board for final approval. Thus, the final budget omits approval by the heads of departments, such as manufacturing (yourself), HR, research, finance and administration.

With the assistance of the latest software, the 12 month budget is prepared. At the end of each month, one month is deleted and another is added. The forecasts assist with assessing the next 12 months. This allows the company to pursue continuous budgeting. Thus, Persaud Products is always budgeting 12 months into the future. This continuous budgeting has become the integral planning and control device for achieving two strategic objectives: ongoing new product development, and rapid continuous improvement.

After the budget is approved by the board of directors and implemented, it becomes the standard against which performance can be measured. This is accepted by all managers in all areas; i.e., they know that their performance will be evaluated by comparing actual results to budgeted results. Despite this understanding, you and your boss, Kim Persaud, have a disagreement on your department's performance during the last month.

In reporting to the board of directors for the first quarter, the CEO praised her own sales efforts for being 20 percent over the sales budget of $25,000,000. In front of the board Kim criticized you for being $1.5 million over your budget (see Exhibit 1).

Exhibit 1

Operating Statement, Manufacturing Department
For the month ending March 31 ($ 000s)

	Actual	Budget	Variance
Variable costs:			
Direct materials	$ 4,576	$ 4,027	549 U
Direct labour	2,924	2,489	435 U
Variable overhead	3,707	3,114	593 U
	$11,207	$ 9,630	1,577 U
Fixed costs:			
Supervisor and manager salaries	$ 1,389	$ 1,400	11 F
Facilities	890	900	10 F
Equipment	765	800	35 F
Other fixed expenses	496	500	4 F
	$ 3,540	$ 3,600	60 F
Total	$14,747	$13,230	1,517 U

You did not say anything at the time. Your manufacturing budget of $13,230,000 was established to accomplish the sales budget of $25,000,000, and you believe that your department exercised effective cost control. All sales were made at the budgeted prices, and all variable costs were transacted at budgeted prices and rates.

Required

Using the case approach, respond to the CEO explaining the performance of the manufacturing department during the last month. Be sure to include suggestions for improving the budgeting process and the use of budgets by managers.

Precious Metals

Just after their December examinations, four management accounting students, who had been team members in a management accounting course, met to consider an equity investment. A relative — a young mining engineer — had asked one member to evaluate a mining proposal, offering him the opportunity to become a shareholder.

This new venture was to mine precious metal on a property that had in the past been considered to have too small of an ore body to be economically viable. Located about 500 kilometres north of Toronto, the mine in question is close to good roads. Moreover, as there is substantial unemployment in the area from the closure of other mines, there are sufficient appropriately skilled workers, with an expected average wage of $22 per hour. Five years ago, when unemployment levels in the province were low, an average wage of $25 might not have attracted the required labour force.

Recent changes in the technology of mining equipment have made economical the mining of smaller properties. Test drilling surveying was done for the property's ore body. The survey concluded that the property has sufficient ore for a mine and processing plant operating for 20 years at 1,500,000 tonnes (1 tonne = 1,000 kilograms) per year. The expected yield is 0.05 percent; i.e., for every tonne there will be 0.5 kilograms of the precious metal.

The mining engineer estimated the equipment and plant at $38 million. Of the total assets, half has a CCA rate of 30 percent, one-third has a CCA rate of 20 percent, and the remaining one-sixth has a CCA rate of 10 percent. The assets will last for the life of the ore body, after which time the expected salvage value is $2 million; only assets subject to 30 percent CCA are salvageable.

The estimated processing costs (excluding amortization or capital cost allowance) are $16 a tonne. Estimated administrative and selling costs are $4 million and $1 million per year, respectively. Working capital requirements are $1 million. An added initial investment of $1 million will recover other trace minerals. This would amount to 100,000 kilograms a year at 10 percent of the kilogram price of the precious metal. Operating costs and other costs would increase by 10 cents a tonne. There is no expected salvage value for these assets, which are in the 30 percent CCA class.

The mining engineer has spent $100,000 for the property, test drilling, incorporation, and solicitation for investors. The company must reimburse her upon start-up. She is also considering the idea of asking $5 million for the company.

The price per kilogram of the precious metal is likely to fluctuate because the metal is a material for luxury goods that varies in demand and price directly with the North American economy. A consulting economist used probability analysis to present estimates of future prices:

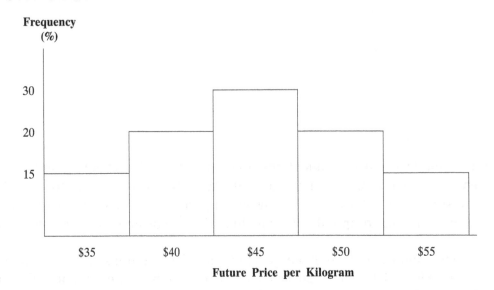

Future Price per Kilogram

Precious Metals would be a typical mining company. Its key success factors would be market price for the metal, yield of the ore, and operating costs per tonne of ore.

There is to be a board of directors to whom the general manager (i.e., the young mining engineer) would report. This board would need to approve the 20-year plan. The board also approves the annual budget and reviews the quarterly performance in comparison to the budget. Otherwise, the general manager has complete autonomy in managing the mine.

The team members have two other concerns: (1) the risk inherent in fluctuations, and (2) that the young mining engineer will run the mine for her benefit and not the owners'. You and your team members had a long discussion about how the owners could be assured that she made decisions best for the company and not just herself. While the team members believed her to be honest, they all believed that differences in objectives could put the interests of the investors in jeopardy.

The discount rate (R) is 8 percent after tax. The income tax (T) rate is 40 percent. Calculate the tax shield with the following equation (C is the CCA rate). For the first year, the half-year rule applies, and it is shown as the second part of the equation.

$$\text{Tax Shield Rate} = \frac{T \times C}{C + R} \times \frac{2 + R}{2(1 + R)}$$

Required

Use the case approach to

1. Evaluate the investment opportunity with a discounted cash flow technique.
2. How would you control the costs in developing the property for production so that the objectives of the owners are being incorporated into decisions and actions?

3. How would you control the general manager after the start of production so that the objectives of the owners are being incorporated into decisions and actions?

CASE 30

Queensview University

You are a management accountant in the controller's department at Queensville University. You have been given the task of calculating the full cost of educating an average student for one class in each of its faculties. The university president assigned the project to your boss, the controller, who requested that you complete the project subject to her review.

Queensville University is typical of many small universities with its senior management structure and range of faculties. Senior management consists of the president, vice-president academic, dean of students, controller, and the deans of the four faculties: humanities, social sciences, physical sciences, and business.

Most of the information needed for calculating the cost per course per faculty is readily available. In the table below you gathered the number of students in each faculty and the total number of courses (i.e., course registrations) taken. In effect, you are required to calculate the cost of delivering an average course in each faculty to a student. The average student takes eight courses each year or, in other words, four courses per term.

| | Faculty | | | | |
	Humanities	Social Sciences	Physical Sciences	Business	Total
Students, #	1,000	1,500	2,000	1,500	6,000
Course registrations, #	8,000	12,000	16,000	12,000	48,000
Rooms booked, #	160	200	400	200	960
Professors, #	32	40	80	40	192
Students per class, #	50	60	40	60	50
Marking costs, $	160,000	360,000	800,000	480,000	1,800,000
Administrative costs, $	200,000	300,000	400,000	300,000	1,200,000

Professors offer classes to deliver courses; this is done in rooms. For each class a room is booked, thus the number "Rooms Booked" equals the number of classes. In addition, for each room booked/class there is a professor to teach the class. Each professor teaches five classes. There are no Internet or blended courses.

There are two other costs. Professors incur marking costs by hiring markers to mark student papers, examinations, quizzes, and assignments. The marking money is provided to each professor, who hires a marker or markers. Administration costs are incurred to schedule professors, classes, and rooms.

Each class is structured for three hours per week in one term. There are two terms a year. Each physical room can be scheduled five days a week during the following four time slots: 9 am to 12 noon, 12 noon to 3 pm, 3 pm to 6 pm, and 6 pm to 9 pm. There are 30 separate rooms. Each room can accommodate classes from any of the faculties. Annual fixed costs for the 30 rooms are $350,000, and the variable costs are $250,000. Each professor is paid $100,000 per year, and his/her time is devoted to the following activities: 40 percent teaching, 40 percent research, and 20 percent service. About one quarter of each professor's service time is devoted to other activities that are to do with students and thus should be included in the cost of delivering classes.

Required

Undertake the project as required. Be sure to specify cost pools and drivers, and related calculations, to determine the cost of delivering a course in each of the four faculties. Be sure to use the case approach.

CASE 31

Quest Manufacturing

You are the management accountant at Quest Manufacturing. Quest has been growing rapidly in the last few years, especially by acquisition of new product lines such as bicycles, children's car seats, small appliances, and furniture. Quest has manufacturing plants around the world, particularly in China and India. Each plant specializes in a limited product line to maximize efficiency.

Quest's customers tend to be large North American and European retail chains such as Wal-Mart and Canadian Tire. These retail chains demand that Quest be responsive to their needs. Quest has achieved high levels of customer satisfaction by fostering excellent relations between its sales representatives and it retail customers. Thus, for example, Quest has placed a permanent, full service account team near Wal-Mart's headquarters in Bentonville, Arkansas. Similarly, Quest has a sales team dedicated exclusively to Canadian Tire.

In the recent year, Quest's sales have increased by more than 20 percent, but profits have declined. Quest is making more products and has more customers, but there is little or no understanding of which customers and products make money and which products and customers lose money. The CEO is very concerned about these losses and wants to know if the management accounting system is able to specify product/customer profitability.

As the management accountant, you provide the CEO with an assessment, or a review, of Quest's present management accounting system. Basically, it is a financial accounting system. Quest's system is able to meet financial reporting requirements and to collect costs accurately by responsibility centres (but not by activities and business processes). In other words, they are adequate for valuing inventory for financial reporting purposes and for preparing periodic financial reports. However, this system produces highly distorted product costs. Relatedly, this system has non-existent or highly distorted customer costs and performance feedback that is too late, too aggregated, and too financial.

The system is able, shortly after the end of the accounting period, to prepare complete financial statements that require minimal post-closing adjustments. Product costing consists of the same simple and aggregate methods used for external financial reporting to value inventory and to measure cost of goods sold. Quest's system has two shortcomings:

- The inability to estimate the cost of activities and business processes and, therefore, the cost and profitability of products and customers; and
- The inability to provide useful feedback to improve business processes.

Required

Using the case approach, you are to advise the CEO on the management accounting systems changes needed to enable Quest to know where it is making or losing money as to products and customers.

CASE 32

RJ Appliance Recycling

Your accounting and consulting firm has been preparing the audited financial statements for RJ Appliance Recycling since its inception two years ago. It is a small but interesting client. As a CPA, you have been hired by this client for a management accounting assignment. You are familiarizing yourself with the company and its business.

Recycling has become a major industry in Canada. Governments, particularly municipal governments, have been active in promoting recycling as a means of reducing demands for landfills. Incentives have been provided to facilitate the establishment of viable recycling businesses.

Two years ago, right after graduation, Raj and John established RJ Appliance Recycling with shop space in an industrial mall on the western outskirts of Ottawa. John's father and Raj's brother became shareholders and board members along with Raj and John. Recycling appliances — such as stoves, refrigerators, washers, and dryers — is the focus of the business.

RJ Appliance Recycling's business model has not changed much in the last two years. Ottawa homeowners and businesses drop off used appliances at the shop. The charge is $20 per appliance, payable by the person disposing of the appliance. This fee is set by the municipality. Once an appliance is received, it is assessed; and based on the assessment, it is sent to one of three possible destinations:

1. Appliances that are newer and in better condition are reconditioned and then sold as refurbished. These refurbished appliances are inventoried and listed at standard (but negotiable) prices for sale. This accounts for about 10 percent of the appliances received.

2. Appliances that are generally working, but not capable of being refurbished, are stripped of useful or good parts. The parts are priced at standard (non-negotiable) prices, inventoried and listed for sale. About 20 percent of the appliances have useful parts. The non-useful components are sorted by type of metal, plastic, etc., and sold for scrap.

3. The other or junk appliances are taken apart, sorted by type of metal, plastic, etc., and sold for scrap. About 70 percent of the received appliances are junked immediately.

Exhibit 1

RJ Appliance Recycling's Net Income Statement — Year 2

REVENUE	
Disposal fees	$300,000
Refurbished appliances	160,000
Appliance parts	140,000
Scrap	105,000
	$705,000
EXPENSES	
Employee salaries, wages, benefits	$310,000
Rent	137,000
Amortization (equipment and vehicles)	14,000
Utilities	31,000
Materials and supplies	35,000
Vehicle expenses (non-amortization)	27,000
Advertisement	24,000
Accounting charges	23,000
Other expenses	23,000
	$624,000
NET INCOME BEFORE INCOME TAXES	$ 81,000

Raj and John — along with one full-time and two part-time employees — assess, refurbish, and strip good parts; then junk remaining partial and full appliances. John developed software for listing the available parts. This web-based listing uses manufacturers' part numbers to facilitate communicating precise parts availability with homeowners and appliance repair shops. As a result, there is a rapid movement of most parts. The inventory records indicate which parts are short of inventory, where there are adequate inventories, and where there are inventories for many years of demand. Consequently, this system enables the stripping of parts to be done with an awareness for inventory levels and sales potential.

Exhibit 1 shows that the second year of business has been profitable. The first year had many startup difficulties, but the second year is more representative of the appliance recycling business. The business model seems to work in general, although the profitability is not satisfactory to the board. You note that employee wages and salaries could be matched with the four revenue streams, but none of the other expenses could be matched with any of them.

The board members are not pleased with overall profitability. They are unhappy that they do not know where the company is profitable and where it is unprofitable. In the future, the board wants the company to be managed more responsibly to ensure a higher level of profitability.

Required

Complete your assignment using the case approach.

CASE 33

Royal Trust

Required

You just joined a major stock brokerage firm. As a condition of your employment contract, you were hired as a research analyst with duties to analyze companies and make recommendations as to whether the shares of certain companies should be bought, held, or sold. Your contract also specified that after one year of experience with the firm, you would become the analyst responsible for banks and financial institutions. On the first day, the director of research asked you to use past annual reports and stock price patterns to explain, with the case analysis approach, the 1993 demise of Royal Trust. He explained that Royal Trust had been a very successful firm over most of its long life, but in a relatively short period of time it ran into problems that were not satisfactorily resolved. You start by gathering together the Royal Trust annual reports for the 1983 to 1992 period, along with monthly stock prices.

The Royal Trust Company ceased operations in 1993. The Royal Bank, an unrelated company, purchased its trust operations and the name Royal Trust; the remaining assets were placed in a new firm called Gentra Inc. This was the end of a 94-year life for Royal Trust; it was also the end of a 10-year period where Trilon Financial Corporation, a financial holding company, was the major shareholder.

In 1983, Trilon Financial Corporation came to own, both directly and indirectly, just over 50 percent of the shares of Royal Trust. Upon acquiring majority ownership of Royal Trust, Trilon installed a new chairman, Mr. J. Trevor Eyton, and a new president and chief executive officer, Mr. Michael Cornelissen.

Chairman Eyton announced two new committees in his 1983 annual report message to shareholders, in addition to the "usual complement of board of directors' committees." The first was the business conduct review committee, which was charged with preparing and monitoring an updated code of business conduct, reviewing business ethics within the company, and resolving any conflict of interest situations applicable to employees, directors, and major shareholders. The directors on this committee were to be independent of the major shareholders, Trilon. The second committee was the investment review committee, which was to consist of seven directors, with the majority being "unaffiliated shareholders directors." The duties of this committee included the review of investment decisions and policies for both client and corporate funds, and any investment decisions involving a major shareholder, affiliated company, or a company with which any director, officer or employee is affiliated.

Although appointed president and chief executive officer only in August 1983, by October of that year Mr. Cornelissen had, according to his message in the annual report, completed a clearly defined and detailed business plan that had been approved by the board of directors. In addition, he announced that

> [p]olicies and objectives for all business segments were defined. Lines of communication have been shortened and simplified to ensure a closeness of senior management to products and services, and to the needs of clients. We have increased our expectations of the standards of performance of our employees and advisors.

If the above were not enough, Cornelissen also announced in the same annual report that there would be a management share purchase plan to commit senior management to shareholder interests:

> The board of directors has approved a share purchase plan and a share option plan subject to approval by the shareholders at the annual meeting. The plans are designed to ensure senior management commitment to the long-term strategic goals and objectives of the company in a manner consistent with shareholder interests.

The annual report for 1984 had Hartland Molson MacDougall give the chairman's report. The previous chairman, Eyton, resigned in October 1984. MacDougall mentioned that Royal Trust had advantages because its parent, Trilon, also owned London Life, Wellington Insurance, and Royal LePage. He did not elaborate on, or explain, these advantages.

Cornelissen's 1984 president's message announced that five important initiatives were undertaken during the past year: (1) a commitment to quality, (2) the arrest and reverse of the past erosion in market share suffered in certain major product lines, (3) a major catch-up with necessary expenditures in computer systems development and marketing, (4) the conservative recapitalization of the company, and (5) the development of a new business planning process. The latter initiative was done by restructuring — i.e., a separation of the company's operations into personal financial services and corporate financial services — in order to be closer to the customer. Cornelissen announced that this would reduce up to five layers of management throughout the company. He also announced six new senior executives, and that an "innovative" employee compensation plan had been designed for implementation in 1985 to "ensure that deserving employees are well rewarded for superior performance against high expectations and standards we set for ourselves." No other details were given.

MacDougall noted in the 1985 annual report that there was a "new Royal Trust" that was bolder and stronger,

> ... with a board of directors who represent the highest standards of business practice and ethics, and a senior management who have established not only clear objectives but also the strategies for achieving our priorities. I am fully confident that the new Royal Trust, with its direct focus on people — our managers, employees, shareholders, and especially, our clients — is well prepared to achieve our goal of being Canada's premier provider of financial services.

Cornelissen's message for the 1985 annual report reiterated his earlier commitment to quality, market focus, and computer systems. He also noted the goal to improve linkages with other members of the Trilon group of companies. He elaborated on the pay for performance programs, which he called "unique." Specifically, he noted that there were three incentive plans — the management incentive option, the employee bonus plan, and the employee share thrift plan — and that they were an integral part of the company's performance management process. Otherwise, few specific details were given about these programs.

MacDougall announced in his 1986 annual report message that the company established a representative office in Tokyo, and, most significantly, acquired Dow Financial Services Corporation. Dow added to the company's asset management and merchant and private banking services in Switzerland, the U.K., Hong Kong and Singapore. Cornelissen announced that the acquisition of Dow more than doubled the company's international operations. He also announced the four major objectives of the current five-year plan: (1) to substantially increase deposits, (2) to double mortgage lending activities, (3) to increase fee income from personal and corporate financial services to 50 percent of net income, and (4) to achieve 15 percent growth in earnings per common share while maintaining conservative capital ratios consistent with high credit ratings. These objectives were to be achieved by investing in technology to create cost-efficient deposit, lending and trust systems; obtaining new and improved branch locations, domestically and overseas; and further exploiting opportunities within the Trilon group of companies. Towards the end of his message, Cornelissen noted succinctly that the expansion would need to come from new sources: "The planned 15 percent earnings growth and 15 to 20 percent return on equity means business growth will have to come, in part, from new and different sources in the years to come."

The most significant part of MacDougall's 1987 chairman's letter was not the content but the quote from a brokerage firm inserted in the margin:

> ...[S]hareholders' interests are shared by senior management whose compensation combines significant share ownership with modest fixed salaries. This arrangement reaffirms management's commitment to long-term earnings growth.

The comment came from an analyst from Walwyn Stodgell Cochran Murray, who apparently favourably viewed the Royal Trust management incentive program for managers. It appears the chairman, MacDougall, thought this approval was important to communicate to shareholders. In other words, the chairman appeared to want to communicate the stock market's approval of Royal Trust's incentive program for managers.

Cornelissen's message stressed the successes of Royal Trust. The quotes in the margin of his president's message communicated what he apparently thought was important. The Canadian Bond Rating Service was quoted as saying:

> [Royal Trust's] primary strength has been their ability to maintain consistent growth in earnings over the past five years while maintaining a quality oriented balance sheet. Throughout this time period profitability ratios have been superior to the industry average despite their conservative leverage ratios and accounting policies.

Andreas Research Capital Inc. was quoted as saying:

> [Royal Trust] management has a sense of purpose and vision of the future and a credible plan to maximize the company's potential that are unparalleled in the

financial services industry in Canada. Moreover, the company's senior management has greater rewards for superior achievement and greater penalties for failure than that of any other financial services company.

On the page following Cornelissen's report, there was a Walwyn Stodgell Cochran Murray quote:

> In 1983, [Royal Trust] brought a new 'entrepreneurial driven' senior management who have concentrated on creating a more productive culture. The company's organizational structure was simplified making it less bureaucratic than it was before and much less than its main competitors, the banks.

MacDougall and Cornelissen announced another good year in the 1988 annual report. The latter explained these good results with the following:

> Royal Trust's sixth consecutive year of record performance again results from the hard work, enthusiasm and energy of our employees. We foster a corporate culture which lets our people's talents and initiatives flourish. The glue that binds us is our shared values. ... We shun hierarchies and bureaucracy. We encourage and reward team players who are willing to take soundly based risks with personal accountability for results. We operate through informal networks and work groups defined by clients' needs rather than internal organization considerations.

This explanation for the successful year was similar to that given by Cornelissen in the prior year. Expansion activities were also described by Cornelissen. This included the introduction of private banking services in Montreal, Toronto, and Vancouver; and new banking, investment and trust operations in Austria, Luxembourg, the British Virgin Islands, the Isle of Man and Barbados. Furthermore, after the year end (February 6, 1989) Royal Trust acquired Pacific First Financial Corporation of Tacoma, Washington in the United States. Cornelissen also reported on the company's performance against objectives. Apparently all objectives had been achieved in the past year.

For the second year, Cornelissen's report included quotes from market watchers. For example, Wood Gundy Inc. was quoted as saying:

> [Royal Trust] is an outstanding, full-service financial services company which should continue to prosper in the de-regulated marketplace. Given the company's strategy and its management's strong personal and financial commitment to company goals, [Royal Trust]'s business fundamentals are excellent.

The Financial Post was quoted as saying:

> Like a well-oiled machine, [Royal Trust] of Toronto continues to produce steady growth in revenue and earnings with enviable consistency.

Instead of a message from the chairman in the 1989 annual report, there was a tribute to him, entitled, "Royal Trust's Secret Weapon." The subtitle read, "Far from using his chairmanship to slow his pace, Hartland MacDougall now works harder than ever." The tribute ended with the following:

> That he is modest about these accomplishments is indicative of a basic humility evident in his every action. He believes honesty and integrity are the most important values in his business. This may explain, in part, his forthrightness.

> Untiring, enthusiastic and personable, Hartland MacDougall is indeed Royal Trust's "secret weapon."

Cornelissen's message to the shareholders summarized the great successes that had occurred for Royal Trust since 1983.

The 1990 annual report had some differences. MacDougall and Cornelissen were now calling themselves, respectively, managing partner, chairman and managing partner, chief executive officer. MacDougall and Cornelissen started the annual report with a "partner tribute," where they admitted that "1990 was the toughest year we have faced since we joined Royal Trust" and that they were proud of "the tireless dedication and loyalty of our employee partners." They then discussed how the "partnership" led "Royal Trusters" to more effectively work together to meet client needs:

> Partnership evolved naturally from our non-bureaucratic, flat organizational structure that allows us to be immediately responsive to client needs. It empowers every partner to break down any barrier that blocks his or her ability to provide superior service. In 1990, partnership changed the way we think about each other and the way we work together.

The 1990 annual report also signalled the use of new terms for describing organizational positions; the traditional job titles of vice-president, director and manager were replaced with managing partner, partner and associate partner. In a section beside the partner tribute, these new titles were described as connoting an individual's level of accountability.

In his chairman's message, MacDougall put the bulk of the blame for poor performance on the "rapidly deteriorating economic conditions in Canada and the United Kingdom." This justification was evident in explaining the problem with the U.K. business:

> Our policy was to be conservative and risk averse. However, some of the loans we made then could not withstand the rigours of a downturn. Skyrocketing interest rates, inflation and a severely depressed real estate market resulted in problem loans for the entire U.K. banking system and we unfortunately were no exception.

In his message, Cornelissen noted that Royal Trust was "solid to the core" and that the loss of $65 million, or $1.20 per share, was the result of several factors: (1) a cyclical economy leading to an increase in mortgage defaults; (2) a combination of prolonged high rates and a steeply depressed property market in the U.K., bringing with it massive loan losses throughout the entire U.K. banking industry; (3) a severe decline in the Japanese stock market that caused investment losses in Switzerland; (4) deterioration in the value of a portfolio of U.S. equities created in 1987 to build relationships with the management of those companies.

In the 1991 annual report, MacDougall noted that 1992 would be a year of opportunity and that it was 100 years since Royal Trust was granted a charter, and 92 years since it opened its first branch. However, he said little about the past year's performance of the company.

Cornelissen said in his message to the shareholders that 1991 was one of the most difficult years for many industries as they experienced the rigours of the worst economic recession since World War II. The year, he said, was devoted to focusing on improving credit controls, reducing expenses, and building on existing strengths. More significant steps were included: restructuring European operations and the discontinuation of certain new construction loans in California. He also included Royal Trust's statement on culture and values, which emphasized entrepreneurial behaviour and adherence to the goals of the owners.

In the annual report for 1992, there was a joint message to shareholders by MacDougall and James Miller, the new president and chief executive officer (the managing partner titles were, apparently, no longer used by the chairman and president). They tersely reported a net loss of $852 million, compared with net income of $107 million for the previous year. On a common share basis, the loss was $5.93. They blamed the losses on economic conditions. They also noted:

> ... the Corporation retained S.G. Warburg to carry out an extensive review of the Corporation's operations and condition and to assist the Corporation, with the co-operation of Trilon Financial Corporation, the Corporation's largest shareholder, in assessing financial alternatives for the Corporation. It was hoped that a major financial institution would be willing to inject substantial new capital into the Corporation and a large number of financial institutions were approached on this basis.
>
> Although a direct investment could not be arranged, the Corporation successfully entered into an Agreement in Principle with Royal Bank of Canada in mid-March, under which Royal Bank has agreed in principle to purchase most of the Corporation's Canadian and international operations. A committee of independent directors has been formed to make a recommendation to the board with respect to the fairness of the proposed transaction to security holders.
>
> The Agreement in Principle with Royal Bank has stabilized Royal Trust's business and has allowed the Corporation to direct its efforts toward regaining some of the business lost during 1992 and early 1993. We firmly believe that the Royal Bank deal was the best deal available to the Corporation and is far better than the alternatives.

With no indication of responsibility or regret, that was the last annual report of Royal Trust.

After reviewing the annual reports, you want to assure yourself that there was a recession in 1990–1992, as stated by MacDougall and Cornelissen in their annual report messages. They had blamed the demise of Royal Trust on the recession. You examine a book from your economics course, *Self-Organizing Economy* by Paul Krugman, which says all of the major industrial countries shared the recessions of 1974–1975, 1979–1982, and 1990–1992. Statistics Canada shows the quarterly growth in gross domestic product in constant dollars for each of those recessions in the table shown in Exhibit 1.

You know that recessions are defined by quarters of negative growth. With only one quarter of negative growth, there was not really a recession during the 1974–1975 period. There were six quarters of negative growth with the 1979 to 1982 recession, and only four quarters of negative growth in the 1990–1992 recession. The data negates the statement by MacDougall and Cornelissen about the seriousness of the 1990–1992 recession.

You notice that there were two main businesses. There was the fiduciary business when Royal Trust was looking after the assets of others. This business showed up as fee and other income on the income statement. As the assets belonged to clients, they were not shown on Royal Trust's balance sheet. The other was the lending business,

Exhibit 1
Quarterly Growth of GDP

Recession	Year	1st	2nd	3rd	4th
1974–1975	1974	1.0	0.3	0.9	0.6
	1975	–0.4	1.1	1.4	0.7
1979–1982	1979	1.1	1.3	0.5	1.2
	1980	0.4	–0.4	–0.9	1.2
	1981	2.5	0.9	–0.7	–0.5
	1982	–0.8	–1.4	–0.9	–0.9
1990–1991	1990	0.7	–0.3	–0.6	–0.9
	1991	–1.3	0.2	0.4	0.3
	1992	0.0	0.2	0.3	0.4

which meant money was raised through deposits and other forms of debt and equity and then loaned or invested in securities, mortgages, loans and other investments. The revenue from this latter business was described as investment income. However, interest expenses and the provision for loan losses were subtracted from investment income to yield net investment income.

You have analyzed the Royal Trust balance sheets and income statements and compiled them in an Excel spreadsheet (as shown Exhibit 2). With your analysis you calculated the margin on investments and gross yield on average funds in use and undertook other analyses (see results in Exhibit 3).

You have also examined the 1983 to 1992 movement of Royal Trust common share prices, on the premise that the efficient market hypothesis predicted that share prices reflected all information about a firm. In other words, the share prices would have reflected important information about the health of a firm that was not contained in the annual reports or otherwise disclosed by the directors. (Exhibit 4 contains the Royal Trust's common share prices from 1983 to 1992.) You discovered that the common share prices of Royal Trust declined to virtually zero in 1993.

Your reading of the annual reports, financial statements, and stock price changes leads you to several opinions contrary to the narrative comments given by the chairmen and presidents and espoused in the annual reports.

Exhibit 2
Financial Statements

Consolidated Balance Sheet
($000,000s)

	1992	1991	1990	1989	1988	1987	1986	1985	1984	1983	1982
ASSETS											
Cash and short-term investments	3,131	3,715	4,958	5,567	5,310	4,279	3,453	2,146	2,070	2,107	2,235
Securities	2,905	5,364	5,470	5,875	3,920	3,616	2,530	1,862	1,621	1,016	1,684
Mortgages, loans, investments	17,790	27,320	29,394	27,475	18,838	16,244	13,068	9,217	7,278	6,344	5,594
Other assets	417	1,127	1,124	909	444	379	295	228	188	167	280
Net assets of discontinued U.S. operations	871										
Total Assets	25,114	37,526	40,946	39,826	28,512	24,518	19,346	13,453	11,157	9,634	9,793
LIABILITIES AND SHAREHOLDERS' EQUITY											
Deposits and debt	22,484	33,798	37,127	36,358	25,906	22,372	17,566	12,010	10,128	9,048	9,248
Other Liabilities, deferred taxes	234	278	280	243	235	271	224	295	226	149	129
Total Liabilities	22,718	34,076	37,407	36,601	26,141	22,643	17,790	12,305	10,354	9,197	9,377
Minority interest	9	8	7	26	42	53	58	17	21	5	6
Subordinated notes and capital debentures	1,419	1,486	1,490	921	661	196	207	—	—	—	—
Shareholders' equity	968	1,956	2,042	2,278	1,668	1,626	1,291	1,131	777	432	410
Total Liabilities and Shareholders' Equity	25,114	37,526	40,946	39,826	28,512	24,518	19,346	13,453	11,152	9,634	9,793

Consolidated Statement of Income
($ millions)

	1992	1991	1990	1989	1988	1987	1986	1985	1984	1983	1982
INCOME											
Investment Income	2,476	3,348	4,916	3,685	2,763	2,218	1,828	1,470	1,204	1,065	1,255
Interest expense	2,124	2,864	3,995	2,907	2,103	1,638	1,351	1,108	987	866	1,061
Net investment income before provisions	352	484	921	778	660	580	477	362	217	199	194
Provision for loan losses	421	155	220	23	18	26	18	12	16	18	13
Net investment income (loss) after provisions for losses	(69)	329	701	755	642	554	459	350	201	181	181
Fees and other income	351	337	349	298	248	200	154	116	263	252	211
Total Income	282	666	1,050	1,053	890	754	613	466	464	433	392
OPERATING EXPENSES											
Salaries and benefits	296	281	369	268	232	187	162	131			126
Premises, computer and equipment	160	154	—	—	—	—	—	—			34
Commissions to real estate brokers/agents	—	—	—	—	—	—	—	—			84
Restructuring costs	—	—	30	—	—	—	—	—			—
Portfolio investments	—	—	84	—	—	—	—	—			—
Other	179	167	461	334	275	233	168	129			101
Total operating expenses	635	602	944	602	507	420	330	260	366	354	345
Other additions	—	—	—	—	—	—	—	—	—	—	3
INCOME (LOSS) BEFORE THE FOLLOWING	(353)	64	106	451	383	334	283	206	98	79	50
Write-off of goodwill	(93)	—	—	—	—	—	—	—	—	—	—
Sale of stock transfer/debt trusteeship businesses	—	21	—	—	—	—	—	—	—	—	—
Income (loss) before taxes, discontinued U.S. operations	(446)	85	106	451	383	334	283	206	98	79	50
Income taxes	213	19	171	186	171	146	129	93	14	18	5
Net income (loss) before discontinued operations	(659)	66	(65)	265	212	188	154	113	84	61	45
Net income (loss) from discontinued operations	(193)	41	—	—	—	—	—	—	1	4	(1)
Non-recurring Items	—	—	—	—	—	—	—	—	—	—	—
Dividends on non-convertible preferred shares	—	—	—	—	—	—	—	35	2	3	—
Dividends on Series A and B convertible preferred shares	—	—	—	—	—	—	—	—	19	10	10
Net income (loss) applicable to preferred shareholders	(55)	71	(86)	74	56	58	51	35	21	13	10
Net income (loss) applicable to common shareholders	(907)	36	(151)	191	156	130	103	78	64	52	34
Net income (loss) after income taxes	(852)	107	(65)	265	212	188	154	113	85	65	44
Average number of shares outstanding (000,000s)	153	145	125	112	105	102	94	83	77	70	70
Earnings (loss) per common share — basic ($)	(5.93)	0.25	(1.21)	1.71	1.48	1.28	1.10	0.94	0.83	0.74	0.49

Exhibit 3
Various Analyses

	1992	1991	1990	1989	1988	1987	1986	1985	1984	1983
Margin (net investment income/investment income)	(0.028)	0.098	0.143	0.205	0.232	0.250	0.251	0.239	0.167	0.170
Gross yield on average funds in use	0.093	0.099	0.144	0.131	0.130	0.125	0.137	0.147	0.148	0.146
Interest cost (including losses)	0.095	0.089	0.124	0.104	0.100	0.094	0.103	0.112	0.123	0.121
Net yield on average funds in use	(0.003)	0.010	0.021	0.027	0.030	0.031	0.034	0.035	0.025	0.025
Rate of growth, securities, mortgages, loans, investments	(0.369)	(0.063)	0.045	0.465	0.146	0.273	0.408	0.245	0.209	0.011

Exhibit 4
Monthly Stock Price Activities ($)

	1992	1991	1990	1989	1988	1987	1986	1985	1984	1983	1982
High price	9.38	11.25	16.13	19.38	17.63	18.50	17.32	11.88	9.20	7.38	5.10
Low price	2.40	7.77	8.13	15.88	12.75	11.00	10.75	8.88	5.94	4.75	2.88
Close for Year	2.94	8.00	9.00	17.88	16.38	13.88	14.82	11.75	9.00	7.38	4.97

Note: Share prices were adjusted in splits.

CASE 34

Royal Wood

Whitby-based Royal Wood is a family owned and operated company, which manufactures solid wood mouldings that are shipped to about 2,000 regular customers throughout Canada and the United States. The mouldings are used in new home construction and renovations. The company's mission is to provide customers with a large selection of quality products with continued support and service. The business was established in 1976, and it has continued to grow successfully for more than 30 years. Its skilled and dedicated workforce along with quality wood products are Royal Wood's strengths. An extensive catalogue is provided of stock items in oak, maple, cherry, poplar and clear and knotty pine.

The president has discussed the purchasing order system with you. (You recently graduated with a CPA, and you are the business analyst with Royal Wood.) All sales to all 2,000 customers are based on purchase orders. Customers prepare paper purchase orders. These orders must be authorized by the customer's purchasing department, and they must be approved by the customer's finance department to verify that funds are available for the purchase. Then the purchase order is mailed or faxed (if there is a rush on the order) to Royal Wood by the customer's mail room.

All purchase orders, whether via mail or fax, are received by Royal Wood's mail room. Subsequently, purchase orders from customers are hand-delivered to Royal Wood's sales department, which checks with the finance department on the credit worthiness of the customer. If the customer has an acceptable credit rating, the sales department approves the purchase order and authorizes the order to be filled by the warehouse. The order is filled by the warehouse and sent to the shipping unit. The shipping unit arranges for delivery to the customer. At the same time, the accounting department is advised by the shipment unit that the order has been shipped. Subsequently, the accounting department requests payments with an invoice sent to the customer.

Upon getting the invoice the customer's mail room sends the invoice to the customer's accounting department for payment. When the shipment arrives from Royal Wood, the customer's receiving unit checks the shipment for completeness and informs the customer's accounting department with a copy of the shipping slip that came from Royal Wood with the shipment. After assurance that the shipment was received for an actual purchase order, the customer's accounting office prepares a cheque to pay for the order. The cheque is sent by the mail room to Royal Wood.

The president says the purchase order process leads to many problems because the paper or fax purchase orders may get lost or delayed at many stages with the customer or with Royal Wood. The passing around of the purchase order is expensive for the customers and Royal Wood. He asks you if the process can be improved through information technology.

Required

Adhere to the president's request by using the case approach to solve the purchase order problems with information technology.

CASE 35

SBS Books

SBS is one of North America's largest book retailers. In the early 1980s it was formed by the amalgamation of two established booksellers that had 90 stores in regional malls. Subsequently SBS expanded into a wider variety of retail outlets. There are now 27 superstores, 800 mall stores, and 85 campus bookstores.

The mall stores are 4,000 to 5,000 square feet each. They are all profitable, but they have little chance of above-average growth. The campus stores are less profitable, but with average profitability they provide advertisement for SBS's other stores. It is the superstores that Dino Giovanni, the president and chief executive officer, expects to provide SBS's growth during the next decade. He is so confident that he changed the firm's name to SBS (for Superbook Stores). And in the last two years, he has experimented with a number of concepts to make the superstores exciting places to be and thereby attractive to customers.

Dino's superstore idea calls for 40,000 square foot destination book stores. Books are sold at discounts of 10 to 40 percent, and each store may have a many as 100,000 titles. Variations to the base store that have been tested include a juvenile book section, a children's book section, a children's activity centre with supervised baby sitting, a restaurant, and an espresso bar. Although stores will vary because of the exact location and premises, the following describes the envisaged superstore:

	sq. ft.
Base store	27,000
Juvenile section increment	4,000
Children's section increment	3,000
Children's activity centre	1,500
Restaurant	3,000
Espresso bar	1,500
	40,000

Real estate is purchased and/or developed to superstore specifications, and then sold to various pension funds. These properties are, in turn, rented. The belief is that SBS can earn above-average return as a book retailer, but property ownership can only yield average returns. Moreover, SBS does not want to tie up its limited financial resources in real estate.

This lack of land and buildings means that there are minimal fixed assets on the balance sheet. The only significant item is leasehold improvement, which individual store managers have no control over. Moreover, cash management, regarding cash balances, accounts receivable, accounts payable, and bank loans, is done entirely by the treasurer. As there is a lack of influence over most balance sheet items, the return on investment (ROI) measure for performance at the store level has come to be calculated as operational income (before interest expenses, corporate allocations, and income taxes) divided by average annual book inventory. Currently, Dino is requiring all aspects of the superstores to earn at least a 20 percent ROI. This demanding target necessitates a skilful blend of profit margin on sales and inventory turnover. There is concern that ROI may not always be appropriate for measuring performance.

As a corporate management accountant, you have been assigned to analyze the profitability of the base store and the variations, and make recommendations to Dino on the size and composition of the superstores and the exclusive use of ROI. You have gathered the following information, which is believed to be representative of future potentials.

Base Store

Sales	$9,450,000
Cost of goods sold	5,670,000
Gross margin	3,780,000
Wages, administration, rent, utilities	3,240,000
Operational income	$ 540,000
Sales to average book inventory	7

Juvenile Section

Revenue	$1,100,000
Cost of goods sold	605,000
Gross margin	495,000
Wages, administration, rent, utilities	445,000
Operational income	$ 50,000
Sales to average book inventory	5

Children's Section

Sales	$ 720,000
Cost of goods sold	432,000
Gross margin	288,000
Wages, administration, rent, utilities	280,000
Operational income	$ 8,000
Sales to average book inventory	4

Children's Activity Centre

Revenue	$ 125,000
Wages, administration, rent, utilities	240,000
Operational income	$ (115,000)

The average charge is $5 per child. On average the parent(s) of each child was found by a survey to have bought $10 worth of books strictly because of the babysitting offered by the children's activity centre. The variable costs of these books are 70 percent of the sales value.

Restaurant

Sales	$ 525,000
Food, supplies	210,000
Wages, administration, rent, utilities	400,000
Operational income	$ (85,000)

The average bill was $9 per customer. On average each of these customers was found by a survey to have bought $10 worth of books strictly because of the restaurant. The variable costs of these books are 70 percent of the sales value.

Espresso Bar

Sales	$ 300,000
Food, supplies	90,000
Wages, administration, rent, utilities	260,000
Operational income	$ (50,000)

The average bill was $6 per customer. On average each of these customers was found by a survey to have bought $15 worth of books strictly because of the espresso bar. The variable costs of these books are 70 percent of the sales value.

Required

As the corporate management accountant, perform the duties assigned by the president. Use the case approach for this assignment.

Singh Brothers Lawn Services

During the summers while you were a university student, you worked at Singh Brothers Lawn Services. The job involved laying sod at new housing developments. It was hard work and long hours, but you enjoyed getting into good physical condition. After having taken an introductory management accounting course in the prior university term, you are becoming more and more critical of the Singh Brothers' management.

The Singh Brothers started the company 40 years ago. They were newly hired high school teachers with lots of energy and ambition, and with summers off. They needed something to do in the summers; and as their father was a developer, business was readily available to them. They soon developed the business beyond their father's development projects to where they were one of the three or four largest sod installers in the province. Lawn installation supplemented the brothers' teaching salaries to where their day jobs paid substantially less than their summer jobs. They had a good life that allowed them to provide for two families and a total of seven children. All of the daughters and sons worked for the company in the past. Now only one son is employed — Satnam, a law student — but there must be six or more grandchildren, and even some other family members. Both of the brothers have retired. The son of one of the brothers, Satnam, now runs the firm.

The business of lawn grass installation consists of laying sod for tracts of new homes. The business has a number of steps. First, developers contact firms that install lawn grass, e.g., the Singh Brothers. The request for proposals comes with plans of housing tracts showing in detail where the grass must be installed, dimensions in square metres of required grass, a date schedule, etc. Generally, a request for proposals has a range of days for laying the grass, usually eight days, but the required time is usually three of those eight days. Second, Satnam bids on jobs that he believes can be done successfully and profitably. Third, with successful bids, a contract is received and the implementation is planned — i.e., the crew is hired and the grass is ordered. Fourth, the grass is installed by the crew according to the contract. Fifth, monies owing for the contract are obtained, and the crew and the grass vendor are paid.

The average contract consists of 70,000 squares metres of grass. There are, on average, 110 contracts in a summer, which runs from early May to late October. Each labourer lays 250 metres per hour. Satnam employs a supervisor for each crew of approximately 10 labourers. Satnam must order grass eight or more working days prior to intended installation.

This has been Satnam's first summer as the person in charge of operations. Previously he was a supervisor, and he sometimes helped his father or uncle. Unfortunately, unanticipated problems have occurred this year. For example, grass was not ordered, the crew was scheduled for the wrong days, and for four contracts the grass was not laid on time. Overall, client satisfaction has decreased. Two contracts were lost when it was obvious to the client that the grass would not be laid on schedule. Some contracts had too many labourers, while other contracts had too few. With two contracts, the crew was at the site, but the grass did not arrive, as it had not been ordered.

Both of the brothers had been able ensure contracts were successfully accomplished to the satisfaction of clients. Satnam has asked you how his father and uncle could have been successful.

Required
With the case approach, advise Satnam.

Southern Computer Machines

Four decades ago, Southern Computer Machines (SCM) started as a manufacturer of semiconductors. However, two decades ago, SCM moved into PC manufacturing as a means of reducing the impact of cyclical semiconductor sales. Now with two successful businesses, analysts at major brokerage firms say the stock market perceives SCM to be only a PC fabricator. The market's perception leads the board of directors to question whether the present divisional structure is the most appropriate for ensuring optimal returns to shareholders' investments. They are sufficiently concerned that they have hired you as a consultant to address the questions of whether the semiconductor division should be (1) kept as currently operated, (2) sold outright, (3) sold through an initial public offering (IPO) to the public, or (4) spun off by distributing the shares to existing shareholders.

You soon learn from a review of the literature and brokerage reports that since its inception, the semiconductor industry has never been able to defy business cycles that swing wildly between boom and bust. Although chip sales have increased at a steady 17 percent rate annually compounded, manufacturing capacity has grown in fits and starts, always lagging behind or exceeding demand. The present boom, which dates back two years, is no exception. For this year, analysts are projecting a 77 percent semiconductor industry-wide profit surge. Until a few weeks ago, most analysts on Bay Street and Wall Street assumed that good times would last two more years, or until chip capacity outpaces demand. Prices would then decline substantially. Nevertheless, short-term indicators were positive. Most chips were in severe shortage, and prices were holding firm or trending up. Simultaneously the Semiconductor Stock Index jumped 68 percent in the six months that ended two weeks ago.

Then, early last week, two Wall Street chip analysts cautioned that the industry could peak within six months. Among the warning signs noted by the analysts were creeping inventory levels, scattered price declines, and shorter waits to obtain some parts. Other Wall Street and Bay Street analysts fired back with counter-arguments, but to little avail; semiconductor stocks fell 20 percent on the Semiconductor Stock Index in the past week. One Bay Street analyst summed up the situation, "This is a cyclical industry, and nobody wants to be the last one out."

With further investigation you see evidence that the investors may have bailed out too early. The industry has changed to where it is no longer as monolithic as it was five years ago, when the semiconductors used in PCs set the pace. The demand has become much more diversified. Now it derives most of its growth from new markets, such as Internet equipment and consumer electronics — everything from data switches and cell phones to digital cameras and DVD players. Consequently, the past extreme cycles are unlikely to be repeated.

The semiconductor industry association has provided some forecasts that indicate attractive future sales. The association says that five years ago, microprocessor and dynamic memory chips, largely used in PCs, provided 39 percent of all semiconductor revenues. In five years from now, the association expects semiconductors for PCs to represent only 25 percent of total sales. The non-PC semiconductors will be the fastest-growing sector, especially those used in communications products and optical parts used with the Internet backbone.

Although the semiconductor division can assume responsibility for a product at any stage of development, OEMs (original equipment manufacturers) benefit most when partnering with the division in the early phases of design. Early involvement with the division's technology solutions, manufacturing and operations, and global services business unit helps to ensure a smooth, rapid and cost-effective transition from product concept to volume manufacturing. Before the division begins manufacturing any product, technology "roadmaps" are established to ensure the best decisions are made. In other words, this process ensures the assembly of functional, quality products that are efficiently manufactured, tested, and serviced.

Depending on the semiconductor product being manufactured, the division's technology solutions business unit is poised to provide a wide range of services, including design of custom-integrated circuits and design co-ordination with the respective OEM. In addition, the division has broad-level design and physical layout capabilities for chip and circuit board assembly. Due to past alliances with router, cell phone, and PC manufacturers, the division now provides a complete array of chips and related products for these market areas.

The fact that the semiconductor division and the PC division are related has created some problems for the semiconductor division. Many potential PC fabricators are reluctant to buy semiconductors from the semiconductor division when they must compete for sales with its sister PC division. Other PC fabricator customers threaten to drop the division because of its association with the PC division. In addition, many of the PC division's major customers perceive there to be an ethical quandary whenever the PC division uses chips from the semiconductor division.

The business model is unclear for the semiconductor division. The division is very good at dealing with suppliers and customers. However, it is merely mediocre with the assembly of semiconductors. This confusion is reflected in its financial performance, depicted in Exhibit 1.

The PC division was started as a means of selling semiconductors. With this purpose, there was a reluctance to becoming a full-fledged manufacturing and sales firm. As a result, the PC division outsourced almost everything, from sales to manufacturing (except for the semiconductors that can be made by the semiconductor division), to research and development. The PC division's business model had invested significantly in supplier assets, which it then linked to its customer assets using the Internet and its organizational know-how and systems. Consequently, the PC division enables customers to access sales and service on its website. Its network of linked suppliers makes it possible for the company to efficiently tailor PC products to fit the needs of individual buyers, whether for a home-based PC for the employees, or with a global company.

Thus, the division was quick to become Web-based for sales and customer service operation. It has no traditional distribution network standing between itself and its cus-

Exhibit 1

Financial Summary — Semiconductor Division

Balance Sheet

ASSETS
Current Assets

Cash, equivalent	$ 543
Net receivables	1,678
Inventories	2,195
Other current assets	326
	4,742

Long-term Assets

Other investments	878
Net property, plant and equipment	4,732
Intangible assets	87
	5,697
TOTAL ASSETS	$10,439

LIABILITIES & OWNERS' EQUITIES
Current Liabilities

Accounts payable	$ 2,146
Accruals	452
Other current liabilities	848
	3,446

Long-term Liabilities and Owners' Equity

Long-term debt	5,249
Deferred income	123
Deferred taxes	223
Other liabilities	56
Owners' equity	1,744
	6,993
TOTAL LIABILITIES & EQUITIES	$10,439

Income Statement

Net sales		$11,757
Less: Cost of goods sold		7,054
Gross income		4,703
Less: Amortization	769	
Selling and administration	3,000	
Total		3,769
Operating income		934
Other income or expenses		(200)
Pre-tax income		734
Income taxes		235
Net income		$ 499

tomers. Customers are served by a telephone or an online order taker who actually works for a division of a telephone company. The order is sent to a co-ordinator — actually an employee who works for another company, Supplyex — who in turn passes the order to the relevant plant from among the division's five assembly plants around the world. At the same time, Supplyex directs parts suppliers of the required parts to the selected assembly plant. Supplyex also directs the parcel courier to the respective plant at the predetermined time to pick up and then deliver the finished computer to the customer.

The division depends on its ability to optimize all assets that make up its business model, including relationships with employees, suppliers, investors, and customers. This clarity of business model is reflected in the PC division's financial performance, depicted in Exhibit 2.

Exhibit 2

Financial Summary — Personal Computer Division

Balance Sheet

ASSETS	
Current Assets	
Cash, equivalent	$ 2,066
Net receivables	1,339
Inventories	196
Other current assets	240
	3,841
Long-term Assets	
Other investments	878
Net property, plant and equipment	382
Intangible assets	66
	1,894
TOTAL ASSETS	$ 5,735
LIABILITIES & OWNERS' EQUITIES	
Current Liabilities	
Accounts payable	$ 1,769
Accruals	168
Other current liabilities	659
	2,596
Long-term Liabilities and Owners' Equity	
Long-term debt	254
Deferred income	135
Deferred taxes	—
Other liabilities	96
Owners' equity	2,654
	3,139
TOTAL LIABILITIES & EQUITIES	$ 5,735

Income Statement

Net sales		$12,632
Less: Cost of goods sold		9,941
Gross income		2,691
Less: Amortization	78	
Selling and administration	1,180	
Total		1,258
Operating income		1,433
Other income or expenses, net		(3)
Pre-tax income		1,430
Income taxes		393
Net income		$ 1,037

After reviewing the semiconductor division, you suggest that the division has to clarify its business model to improve performance. It does not focus on what it does best.

Required

As the consultant, specify how the semiconductor division can clarify its business model and improve profits. Also, specify the advantages and disadvantages from each of the following options: (1) keep as a division, (2) sell outright, (3) sell through an initial public offering (IPO) to the public, or (4) spin off by distributing the shares to existing shareholders.

Upper Canada Wood Stoves

This is your first assignment as a consultant with the prestigious McHenry Consulting firm. You want to do well. Three years ago you graduated with a business degree, and last month you earned your CPA designation. McHenry hired you last week; and after getting familiarized with McHenry's business model and practices, you have been assigned to a new client, Upper Canada Wood Stoves.

Upper Canada Wood Stoves was established in 1810 as a family business. It was a booming business for its first century, but during the 20th century sales declined with the replacement of wood stoves with oil, natural gas, electricity, and central heating. Actually, the company nearly disappeared on more than one occasion. For the last two decades, the company produced only one model, called the Traditional Canadian wood stove. With this improvement in business, the owners saw an opportunity for a more contemporary model, called the Airtight Canadian. This new model is focused on customers using wood, at their cottages and country homes, as an alternative source of energy for cooking and heating.

In each of the first three years on the market, Airtight's sales met expectations. Company profits were, however, less than expected. It was unclear if the Airtight stoves were really profitable.

Sales for the latest year, shown in Exhibit 1, were for 15,000 traditional stoves at $1,000 each and 1,000 airtight stoves at $3,500 each. The company had calculated profitability in its normal method, as shown in Exhibit 2. The new airtight stoves were, accordingly, an outstanding success. On the other hand, profitability of the traditional stove had become dismal, which was difficult for the CEO to understand as it had been considered a successful stove up until the introduction of the airtight stove.

The results, in Exhibit 2, were being questioned by the CEO. She recognized that profitability per stove had always been determined by gross profits per stove, i.e., by dividing the company's gross profits by the number of stoves sold.

The CEO had considered raising the price of the traditional stove to improve profits, but had delayed that decision for two reasons. First, the traditional stove was already competitively priced in its market. Market research had indicated that price increases would be met with even larger declines in units sold. Second, she wanted to get advice on product costing and product profitability. In the past, with one product, it was obvious that product profitability was synonymous with the company's profits.

However, with two products the CEO thought that a new method might be needed for product costing and for determining product profitability. Consequently, your consulting firm was engaged.

After reviewing Exhibits 1 and 2 and understanding the CEO's concerns, you realized that more cost information is needed, and you in detail asked for and received the information contained in Exhibits 3, 4, 5.

Exhibit 1

Income Statements for Traditional and Airtight Stove
June 30 ($ 000s)

REVENUE	$18,500
COST OF GOODS SOLD	
Direct materials	6,800
Direct labour	2,400
Factory overhead	5,800
	15,000
GROSS PROFIT	3,500
SELLING AND ADMINISTRATION	
Selling	1,200
Administration	1,000
	2,200
NET INCOME BEFORE TAXES	$ 1,300

Exhibit 2

Profitability Analysis, Per Stove

	Traditional Stove	Airtight Stove
Revenue	$1,000.00	$3,500.00
Cost of goods sold*	937.50	937.50
Gross margin	$ 62.50	$2,562.50

* $15,000,000/16,000

Exhibit 3

Direct Costs Per Stove

	Traditional Stove	Airtight Stove
Direct materials	$400	$800
Direct labour	8 hours of unskilled labour at $15 per hour	24 hours of skilled labour at $25 per hour

Exhibit 4

Factory Overhead, by Activity

Activities	Costs	Cost Driver
Material related	$1,500,000	These costs are associated with the administration and physical movement of parts around the factory. The number of parts in each stove, traditional and airtight, was 20 and 40, respectively.
Labour related	1,300,000	Overhead costs (such as utilities, equipment depreciation, etc.) that are incurred to support the time consuming activities of cutting, welding, sanding, assembly, and packaging.
Paint Setup	800,000	Traditional stoves were made in batches of 3,000; airtight stoves were made in batches of 200 stoves. The number of setups drove these costs.
Painting	1,400,000	Painting costs were incurred equally per stove.
Human resources	800,000	Number of people employed in production drive human resource administration and benefits.
	$5,800,000	

Exhibit 5

Other Overhead

Activities	Costs	Cost Driver
Selling	$1,200,000	It was estimated that 10 percent of these costs were incurred for the traditional stoves, while 90 percent were incurred for the airtight stoves.
Administrations	$1,000,000	It was estimated that each brand — traditional and Airtight — uses 10 percent of these resources. The remaining 80 percent supports the overall company.

Required

Use the case approach to address the CEO's requirements. Be sure to explain your analyses and recommendations.

Yoour University

Your first job was with Barnard Bensen LLP. Although you were hired to pursue a CPA to become a licensed professional accountant, you decided after a week that your preference was for enterprise business systems technology and strategic financial management. Consequently, you obtained your CPA designation with a specialty in performance measurement and financial accounting and sought all possible enterprise business systems technology assignments, especially those involving front end, customer-facing applications, such as customer relationship management (CRM). Now you are a manager at Barnard Bensen in the customer solutions practice.

CRM systems and other related software allow organizations to automate and increase the efficiency of their front offices by making all contact information explicit. The front office deals with an organization's acquisition, retention, and interaction with customers, as opposed to the back office or the behind-the-scenes systems, which deal with production, logistics, administration, and accounting. These back office systems are powered by enterprise resource planning systems, such as PeopleSoft and SAP. Customer-facing applications ensure that staff on the front lines have easy access to customer histories, interactions, and transactions. They also provide customer self-service capabilities through interactive voice, data, and Internet channels. Specialist CRM software links together all of these parts of the business and allows staff at all levels of the organization to see up-to-the-second customer information on a continuous basis.

A customer database or, more precisely, a data warehouse accompanies CRM systems. Data warehouses contain all customer information to support real-time analyses that assist in managing the customer relationship at all touch points or points of interaction with customers — Web, telephone, e-mail, and face-to-face, plus point-of-sale, billing, or other operational systems — both inbound and outbound. CRM makes sure that all customers are treated the same, regardless of how they are interacting with the organization. For example, if a customer contacts a call centre with a service complaint, the call-centre representative can see that the customer has a large order pending and expedite the order to keep the customer satisfied. In this way, CRM is called database marketing.

Specifically, the CRM data warehouse contains details on customers, names, addresses, when and what they have purchased, when and why they have contacted the organization, how they have responded to advertisements and promotions, etc. A data

147

warehouse should have all information on all customers, and ideally it should maintain information on prospective customers as well as past customers.

CRMs are important for three reasons. First, customers are an organization's most valuable asset. Each customer on the list is expensive and time-consuming to acquire. Past customers are the most likely to be future customers. Second, most organizations do a poor job of dealing with customers. This is usually because the organization is unable to co-ordinate all of its customer touch points. Third, the Internet and information technology allow for a much greater proportion of customer interactions to be captured, co-ordinated, and delivered digitally.

Amazon.com provides an example of an organization using a CRM system. Amazon users browse the website, then order books and CDs using formatted Web pages by filling in order, personal and credit card details. Amazon's system captures all of this data, using it to push recommendations based on customers' buying histories. Customer files are used to automatically send e-mails on the status of orders, and to mass-market new services like auctions. Furthermore, if customers are browsing travel books on, for example, Jamaica, Amazon's system can flash up a recommendation for a Bob Marley CD, with one-click ordering. Moreover, Amazon has a complete record of a customer's e-mails and its own responses. Amazon also collects data on which promotions work and which do not.

CRM systems allow organizations to collect and analyze customer data and, in some cases, initiate real-time responses. Older CRM software packages or operational applications are limited to gathering data from customer interactions such as service calls, sales transactions, and website activity. The newer CRM software packages include analytical applications that evaluate customer data for patterns that assist with the development of marketing campaigns and targeted sales pitches. CRM systems are able to integrate all touch points, whether telephone, Internet, or personally initiated, and notes from academic advisors. Information for the latter is the most difficult to capture, as it often is manually inputted.

Banks are using CRM systems to put personalization back into the banking relationship. Twenty-five years ago banking was personal, face-to-face, and largely conducted in the branch. Then, through the introduction of cost-reducing automatic teller machine (ATM) technology, customer closeness was lost. Banks were able to further reduce costs by automating more transactions, but at the cost of being detached from customers. Banks use CRM technology to efficiently and effectively understand customer requirements and to respond to problems. However, banks need to be careful that the CRMs are not used primarily for cross selling other bank services.

You are the manager assigned to write the proposal for implementing a CRM (customer relationship management) system at Yoour University, the major university in the capital city where you live. You learn from the partner in charge of the information technology practice that the request for proposals (RFP) has come from Yoour University's president, who sees a need to change the way students and the university interact with administrative matters. In the RFP, there are three reasons underlying the president's desire for a CRM system. First, a CRM would reduce costs from the multitude of overlapping and expensive systems that currently provide incomplete service to students. Evidence from Dell Computer estimates — costs per customer service interaction as $10 with personal contact, $7.50 with call centres, $2.45 with voice response systems, and $0.18 with Internet — have influenced the president in her desire for a CRM system. Second, a CRM system would provide students with improved services by having a co-ordinated focus to their inquiries and transactions with the university. Third, improvements in the student experience would instill positive feelings, thereby leading them to be better alumni donors after they graduate. Your task is to detail the scope and components that are part of the CRM system. With that description, the president can contact CRM vendors for quotations for an installed CRM system.

At a meeting arranged by the president to provide information to consulting organizations interested in submitting proposals, you learn that Yoour University has 35,000 undergraduate students and 10,000 graduate students. Back office activities are handled by an enterprise resource planning system by PeopleSoft. For the front office activities dealing with students and the focus of CRM, Yoour University has the following computerized or manual systems.

1. **Admissions.** The Admissions unit is responsible for obtaining enrolments. This is done by first recording all applicants and then accepting those who qualify, according to established criteria. This responsibility also involves communications with applicants by mail, telephone, and e-mail. It also assigns accepted students with unique identifying numbers. Manual forms are used with the admissions process.

2. **Registrar.** This unit keeps track of student academic progress with what is called the student information system. It records all grades, grade changes, reactivations, faculty transfers, course adds, course drops, etc. It interacts with students using the voice response system, the Web page, e-mail, surface mail, and telephone. The registrar unit also does a program audit once students have declared they expect to graduate, which is either at the spring or fall convocation.

   One shortcoming was noted: the student information system does not do prerequisite checks to ensure that students have the proper background for the courses they are taking. Also, a new website was launched to bring under one umbrella all existing interactive services for students. These services include not only the capacity to change an address or SIN, but also to view grades and student accounts.

   Presently, the admissions unit and the registrar's unit are located in separate buildings across campus from each other. There are plans to place both under the same roof to improve services to students.

3. **Transcripts.** Current and past students contact the registrar's unit for certified copies of their transcripts. Name and address information is not used to update student or alumni records.

4. **Financial assistance.** This unit has primary responsibility for all aspects of a student's financial relationship with the university, including administration of provincial assistance, allocation of bursaries and scholarships, and the collection of fees. There are a number of systems involved. Recently, this unit developed a new student account statement and made it available on the Web. It also implemented Internet and telephone banking to make it easier for students to make their payments to the university without having to wait in a lineup.

5. **Residence.** Each student in residence is recorded in the residence system. The data collected include name, home address, next of kin in case of emergency, and room/apartment assignment. Also, there is a system that looks after recording the payment of various residence fees.

6. **Faculty.** Each faculty, such as Arts, Education, and Business, answers questions posed by students regarding their programs or courses, required electives, location of classes, dates for final examinations, etc. Generally this is done by

a specialized unit, commonly called the office of student assistance and services. Students also contact the dean, associate dean or an administrative person on these matters. Some faculties have, on their own, established Web pages to proactively address student questions and concerns.

7. **Departments.** Each department has administrative personnel who answer questions posed by students regarding their program or courses required, electives, location of classes, dates for final examinations, submission of assignments, etc. To be proactive, some departments have established Web pages to address student questions and concerns.

8. **Alumni.** Once students graduate, they automatically become members of the Yoour University alumni. Although the names of all graduates are correctly recorded along with the degree or degrees, the addresses have not been accurately maintained. A few years ago, an organization was allowed to contact or, more often, attempt to contact all possible alumni in order to compile an alumni directory. The company was allowed to sell the directory. Yoour University benefited from up-to-date addresses for many alumni members. However, at the termination of the project, addresses were listed for only about half of the graduates, and many of those addresses were incorrect. Other than this arrangement, Yoour University has not, before or after, attempted to systematically keep track of its alumni. It is estimated that only 35 percent of the addresses are correct.

9. **Advancement.** Fundraising is done, or at least co-ordinated, by the Advancement unit. Careful records are maintained of all donors. This list is used for regular fundraising activities, following the argument that the best donors are those who have donated in the past.

10. **Library.** A separate record of all persons with library cards is maintained. This list is automatically updated with changes in the status of students, faculty, or staff. Alumni members are allowed to obtain library privileges at a nominal annual charge.

Required

In order to prepare a proposal for designing an effective CRM system or systems, first identify the existing systems and document what they do; then design for Yoour University a CRM system or systems to address what should be done. Use the case approach.